SOLVING LIFE'S PROBLEMS

Methods of The Master

By Hillyer Hawthorne Straton

THE BETHANY PRESS
ST. LOUIS, MISSOURI

Books by the same author:

PETER, THE MAN JESUS MADE
BAPTISTS: THEIR MESSAGE AND MISSION
THINKING WHERE JESUS THOUGHT
PREACHING THE MIRACLES OF JESUS

Scripture quotations, unless otherwise noted, are from the *Revised Standard Version of the Bible,* copyrighted 1946 and 1952 by the Division of Christian Education, National Council of Churches, and used by permission.

Printed in the United States of America

To
SYLVIA AND CARTER
Daughter and Son, Beloved
Who along with all of us have been a part of the problem,
but are fast becoming a part of the solution.

Preface

Every generation thinks its problems are the most momentous. Try for a moment to place yourself back in the 1850's in the United States and see if you could figure out a solution for the slavery issue. Yet problems for our age seem peculiarly annoying, for at the very time when we have conquered so much of our physical environment we are plagued with difficulties in human relations that baffle us. Perhaps God in His infinite wisdom is allowing this present frustration to drive us back to Him and to His way for us.

There are various ways to face the problems of life. A few can retreat to a Magic Mountain or a Shangri-La. Others take up every moment with perpetual "busy-ness." Too many find surcease in the anodyne of alcohol. The best solution is that which men of faith through the ages have found in their own lives to give the peace that passes all understanding. It is faith in the ultimate goodness of God and His mercy toward all men. Answers are never facile and we would not make them so. The Christian, however, finds major help in the Gospels. Jesus never promised his followers ease, rather the otherwise; they would have certain benefits but the pregnant phrase is added: "with persecution."

But he did promise his presence, and this has always been more important than freedom from trial.

No attempt is made in this volume to answer all the problems of life. Some of the major issues you and I must face are considered. Jesus almost never wraps up the solution in a neat package; rather, he points the direction. Yet it is never a path out there in the dim unknown. It is a Way where his feet have trod. "Follow me . . . you should do as I have done."

My thanks are due to Miss Florence McIntire for her secretarial help, to Robert Torbet, to Francis Whiting for his excellent cover and title suggestions, also to Victor Scalise, Murray Ford, Eugene Dolloff, and Louis Keating for their help in title and chapter headings.

HILLYER H. STRATON

Study: First Baptist Church
Malden, Massachusetts

CONTENTS

Acknowledgments

The author wishes to thank the following publishers and individuals for permission to use copyrighted material:

ASSOCIATION PRESS, for quotation from *Creative Society*, by John Macmurray.

NATALIE BIGELOW, for "Guilty" by Marguerite Wilkinson.

CHRISTIAN CENTURY FOUNDATION, for "Prayer for the Nations" by Marjorie Farmer, *Christian Century*, November 13, 1946; for a quotation from Paul Elmer More, *Christian Century Pulpit*, December, 1945; for portions of "How My Mind Has Changed in the Past Decade" by Hillyer H. Straton, *Christian Century*, October 26, 1949; and, for "Guilty" by Marguerite Wilkinson.

CHAPPELL AND CO., INC., for "Carefully Taught" from *South Pacific*, by Richard Rodgers and Oscar Hammerstein. Copyright 1949 by Williamson Music, Inc. Used by permission.

CAMBRIDGE UNIVERSITY PRESS, for quotations from *Christian Doctrine*, by J. S. Whale, and *The Teachings of Jesus*, by T. W. Manson (also permission of Dr. T. W. Manson).

JAMES CLARKE AND CO., LTD., for an excerpt from *The Parables of Jesus*, by A. T. Cadoux.

THOMAS CURTIS CLARK, for his poem, "All praise to thee, our country."

DETROIT FREE PRESS, for excerpts from the editorial, "Greater Love Hath No Man," which appeared December 4, 1942.

DETROIT NEWS, for quotations from Edgar DeWitt Jones's column, "Successful Living," of January 12, 1944.

FEDERAL (now NATIONAL) COUNCIL OF CHURCHES, for excerpts from *The Christian and His Occupation*, by J. H. Oldham.

HARCOURT, BRACE AND COMPANY, INC., for excerpts from

8

The Rock, by T. S. Eliot, copyright, 1934, by Harcourt, Brace and Company, Inc.; and from *Abraham Lincoln: The Prairie Years,* by Carl Sandburg.

HARPER AND BROTHERS, INC., for excerpts from *Our Eternal Contemporary,* and *Can Christianity Save Civilization?* by Walter M. Horton; from *The Great Century,* and *Christian Outlook,* by Kenneth S. Latourette; from *God's Grace and Man's Hope,* by Daniel D. Williams; and, "My Yoke Is Easy" by Gladys Latchaw, and "Courage" by Amelia Earhart, from *Masterpieces of Religious Verse,* edited by James Dalton Morrison.

LITTLE, BROWN AND COMPANY, for an excerpt from *Yankee from Olympus,* by Catherine Drinker Bowen.

LONGMANS, GREEN AND COMPANY, INC., for quotations from *The Varieties of Religious Experience,* by William James.

OXFORD UNIVERSITY PRESS, INC., for excerpts from *Study of History,* by Arnold Toynbee; and Kierkegaard: *The Journals.*

PRINCETON UNIVERSITY PRESS, for quotation from Paul Elmer More.

G. P. PUTNAM'S SONS, for "Courage," by Amelia Earhart.

RANDOM HOUSE, INC., for "Holes in the Sky," by Louis MacNeice.

CHARLES SCRIBNER'S SONS, for portions of "The Toiling of Felix" from *The Poems of Henry Van Dyke; Christian Realism,* by John Bennett; *God and the Common Life,* by Robert L. Calhoun; "If This Were Faith" in *Poems and Ballads,* by Robert Louis Stevenson; *Revelation and Response,* by E. P. Dickie; and, *Christianity as History and Faith,* by A. C. McGiffert.

WORLD COUNCIL OF CHURCHES, for an excerpt from *Interseminary Series,* III, by E. G. Homrighausen.

ZONDERVAN PUBLISHING HOUSE, for a quotation from *The Kingdom of God and the Son of Man,* by Rudolph Otto.

Life's Basic Realities . . .

CHAPTER ONE

Your Religion and Jesus

Augustine Birrell said of the Brontë sisters living
in the Yorkshire rectory that only Anne had enough
religion to give her pleasure. A corollary which
has been recognized is that there are many people
who have enough religion to make them feel un-
comfortable when they do wrong but not enough
to make them feel good when they do right. At
some time or other, religion is a problem which you
have to face. The manner in which you face it often
determines destiny.

We would expect that the attitude of Jesus toward religion would be normative. It was as fresh
and healthy as was his every reaction toward large
life. Along with every good first-century Hebrew,
religion was central to Jesus. The whole of his life
revolved around religious attitudes. If a good Jew
of that period could be transported to the twentieth
century, he would be completely baffled at our dis-
tinction between secular and sacred, for to him
everything would be religious in the best sense of
the word. The religion of his ancestors permeated
the life of our Lord. He lived, breathed, and had
his being in fellowship with God, his Father. Jesus
knew his Bible, our Old Testament scriptures. It

11

was divided in his day into three great areas: the "law," the "prophets," and the "writings." He knew it as few have ever known it.

This knowledge of the Word of God was a type of education that was unsurpassed. The wisest of men are not always those who have attended universities. Nicholas Murray Butler was on an ocean voyage with Will Rogers. He was so greatly impressed with the sagacity and wisdom of the cowboy humorist that he offered him an honorary degree from Columbia University. Will replied, "Well, Nicholas, I knew you gave degrees for all kinds of ignorance, but not for my kind of ignorance!" Yet Will Rogers was among the wisest men our country has produced. Though Jesus did not have rabbinical training, which was the formal higher education of his period, yet "no man ever spoke like this man." The written word of God, coupled with his own inward understanding of the will of God, supplied our Lord with a knowledge that gave him surpassing wisdom.

Prayer was always a major factor in the religious observance of Jesus. Our Lord knew what it meant to commune with God. Again and again we find him slipping away for long hours of prayer; on the mountainside, in the garden, or lifting his soul and voice briefly in a busy ministry. His was a constant attitude of prayer. "Father, I thank thee that thou hast heard me." (John 11:41.) It was prayer for others. It was prayer that God would help him to help them. His prayers were in complete contrast to the farmer who prayed, "O Lord, bless me, my wife, our son, John, and his wife. Us four and no more!"

Worship, a vibrant reality to Jesus, was a matter of the spirit. To a woman at a well in Samaria Jesus said, "Neither on this mountain nor in Jerusalem will you worship the Father. . . . But the hour is coming, and now is, when the true worshiper will worship the Father in spirit and truth." (John 4:21, 23.) If our present generation is to be saved, God must be worshiped not only in foxholes and rubber rafts or in great churches and cathedrals, but also in the marts of business, the halls of learning, the roar of factories, the seats of government, and the council tables of empires. There is evidence that Jesus would have had as little use for prayer to get one out of a fix as he had for those who followed him for the loaves and fishes. He refused to turn stones into bread to supply even a genuine physical need for himself.

Religious observances were far more than perfunctory in the life of our Lord. He was careful to observe, and evidently delighted in, the major outward worship customs of his day. As a lad he had thrilled to be "in my Father's house," for he had been drilled by Joseph and Mary to believe that the Temple at Jerusalem was the center of all religious observances. This ultimate loyalty to the Temple and its worship was dramatized by the hot wrath with which he drove out the money-changers (Mark 11:15f), who were making his Father's house a house of merchandise. Jesus felt close to God everywhere, but especially in his Father's house. Albert Schweitzer tells of an old man who was stone deaf and yet never missed a service of worship in the church where Schweitzer's father was the minister. When asked what he got out of the service he replied, "The communion of the saints; the communion of the saints."

At the stated periods of worship in the synagogue we find Jesus in his place. "And he came to Nazareth where he had been brought up; and he went to the synagogue, as his custom was, on the Sabbath day." (Luke 4:16.) What a wealth of meaning is in the phrase, "as his custom was." There is a good deal of evidence that Jesus would have little patience with his followers who could come to church only on special occasions like Easter and Christmas. If Jesus needed and received value from the strength of worship, how much more do you need it!

Look for a moment at the reaction of Jesus to arbitrary religious prohibitions or taboos. Taboos are not always to be despised, because many of them have actually had a purpose. Primitive people may not have understood why marriage was forbidden between close relatives, though we today know that such a provision was eminently wise to prevent the transmission of inherited weaknesses.

In the days of our Lord, sabbath taboos had become a plague.

Jesus put the day of rest and worship back into its rightful place. The sabbath was made for man, not man for the sabbath. If his disciples were hungry on the sabbath it appeared sensible to him, and in keeping with the ultimate design of God, for them to satisfy their hunger by plucking grain in the field and rubbing it out (threshing) in their hands. Such laxity was a scandal to the warped legalists of his day. They had taken God's wise command for sabbath observance and made a narrow taboo of it. Jesus did not hesitate to incur the enmity of such small-hearted religious leaders when the real needs of men were at stake.

The separated life has been a shibboleth with a certain type of Christian. It usually involved prohibition against card-playing, dancing, and theater-going. The extremes to which such attitudes can reach are well illustrated in an early pastorate of the present author. The wife of one of my deacons took serious objection to a social occasion for the young people of the church held in the parsonage. When she was asked why, she replied that the pastor served ginger ale! When pressed further and asked what was the matter with ginger ale, she said that ginger ale comes out of a bottle and has the appearance of evil. The wise wife of another deacon came back at her: "Why, Mary Jones, every one of your babies was raised on a bottle!" Jesus taught that separation must be a matter of morality, not of taboos. "Go and learn what this means, 'I desire mercy, and not sacrifice.'" (Matt. 9:13.) You can never build a warm, appealing, vigorous religion on taboos, on "thou shalt nots." This was one of the reasons why Paul broke with organized Judaism, and stood for the liberty which he found in Christ.

Observe again how closely Jesus connected morality and religion. Once religion had nothing to do with morality—if you obeyed the regulations you could live as you pleased. (This is a view that has not been entirely lost.) We have to thank the genius of the Hebrew religious leaders for binding religion and morality forever together. Jesus said, "Out of the heart are the issues of life," and "not what goes in but what comes out of a man defiles him"; as Browning well said: "Religion's all or nothing."

Jesus constantly went back to the moral law that underlay his Father's world. On one occasion a delegation came to Jesus to try and trap him with a question about divorce, reminding him that Moses had allowed it. Lax divorce attitudes were a problem in some circles then, even as today. The school of Rabbi Hillel taught that a man could divorce his wife for so slight a cause as burning his food. In passing, notice the innate goodness of Jesus. When they asked him the question *they knew what his answer would be.* They tried to trap him by his large-

heartedness. Jesus immediately went back of Moses
to the moral law. "For your hardness of heart
Moses allowed . . . but from the beginning it was
not so . . ." (Matt. 19:8). Jesus recognized pro-
gressive revelation and the times of ignorance which
God winked at. He was aware that back of every
religious injunction stands the great moral law.

There is wisdom here for the modern Christian.
You must be against a certain evil not because the
Bible does or does not condemn it, but because it is
intrinsically wrong. This was the principle of Jesus.
For instance: the Bible says nothing about gambling
except possibly by implication. As a modern Christian you know that it is evil because you stand on
the firm ground of natural or moral law. Gambling
is wrong because it deprives a man of his property
rights without adequate compensation.

Finally, we discover Jesus putting both repentance and forgiveness at the very heart of religion.
Here is the only basis on which right relations can
be restored between God and man, and man and
man. Jesus set the example of divine forgiveness
by his own atoning death on the cross. "Father,
forgive them; for they know not what they do."

Jesus gave us a religion that works. You and I
must share a working religion with those who do
not possess it. One of the most dramatic instances
of the sharing of the religion of Jesus is in the case
of a traveling man by the name of L. R. Graves.[1]

[1]*Christian Century Pulpit*, August, 1942.

Years ago he spoke to his friend, Samuel M. Sayford, and kept his name on a private prayer list. Sayford became the secretary of the Evangelistic Association of New England and led C. K. Ober, a student at Williams College, to Christ. In Cornell University Mr. Ober found and influenced John R. Mott, who was struggling over the problem of his lifework. Mott chose Christian service as his career with emphasis on ministry to youth. The result of Mott's choice is endless, for he has influenced more young men and women to choose Christian callings in the world field than any other man. It was a religion that worked for Graves, Sayford, Ober, and Mott. It worked for Jesus and it will work for you.

Life's Basic Realities . . .

CHAPTER TWO

Your Life's Meaning and Jesus

Phrases are characteristic of ages: "Know thyself" immediately calls to mind the Greece of Socrates, 465 B.C. "The just shall live by faith," speaks of Martin Luther and 1525. "Life, liberty, and the pursuit of happiness" is the watchword of 1776. "That government of the people, by the people, and for the people shall not perish from the earth," recalls the immortal Lincoln. "Make the world safe for democracy" and "Open covenants, openly arrived at," echo the aspirations of millions on the lips of Woodrow Wilson in 1917-1918.

The Bible is not a naive book. It uses the phrases, the language of its own day, but it is remarkably modern in its outlook. Men in the Bible want to be shown just as much as in any modern scientific laboratory. We find Thomas saying, "Unless I see in his hands the print of the nails . . . I will not believe." On another occasion he asked Jesus, "How can we know the way?" In response the author of John's Gospel has Jesus sum up in a phrase the ultimate search for meaning that is at the heart of Christian faith. "I am the way, and the truth, and the life; no one comes to the Father,

19

but by me." Alfred North Whitehead once said, "That religion holds the future which shows the eternal down among the facts." How does this word of Jesus stand in the light of such an observation from a world-famous philosopher?

This section of John's Gospel is a part of what we know as the farewell discourse of Jesus. Our Lord is shortly to leave the upper room and go out to his arrest and death. These words are used so often in times of sorrow that we overlook the context. Yet John 14 is just as significant for life as it is for death. Observe that Jesus is here cheering the disciples rather than being cheered by them. The only remotely comparable scene is in Plato's immortal *Phaedo* where Socrates, before drinking the hemlock, encourages his sorrowing disciples. So the first movement of the discourse begins, "Let not your hearts be troubled; believe in God, believe also in me" and ends, "And you know the way where I am going." Jesus had spent his whole ministry trying to instruct his disciples in his way. Yet Thomas responded, "Lord, we do not know where you are going; and how can we know the way?" Observe how modern is the query of Thomas. It has been well said that because of the doubts of Thomas we can believe. To this question Jesus responded, "I am the way, and the truth, and the life; no one comes to the Father, but by me." This statement involves three fundamental human needs, guidance: "I am the way"; instruction: "I am the truth"; provision: "I am the life." It closes with the most challenging absolute ever uttered, "No one comes to the Father, but by me." These words involve the most arrogant assumption ever spoken or they are words of eternal reality. Even if you say that the Gospel author is here interpreting rather than reporting, it is still a testimony that Jesus was such a person that this could be believed to truly represent his position. Now a question moderns are still asking is, "Do we have the ultimate answer in this reply of Jesus?" Let us look at it for a moment.

I. Guidance—I AM THE WAY

Notice the biblical usage of the term "way." In the Old Testament: "Thus says the Lord: Behold, I set before you the way of life and the way of death" (Jeremiah 21:8). "Your ears shall hear a word behind you, saying, 'This is the way, walk in it'" (Isaiah 30:21). In the Gospels: Matt. 7: 13-14 has "the way is easy, that leads to destruction ... the way is hard, that leads to life." In Acts 9:2 Paul journeys to Damascus to arrest "any belonging to the Way." In 18:25 is the statement, "He had been instructed in the way of the Lord." Now a *way* is a road to walk upon but just as often it is a sign to point the direction. There are two metaphors: *Jesus is the highway itself*. This is not out of keeping. In Canada the main routes of travel are often called "The King's Highway." Roads are always the symbol of the tying together of life. You remember a popular book of a few years ago entitled, *The Roadmenders.* Isaiah says, "Make . . . in the desert a *highway* for our God." Men need the physical bond that will tie them together, and Jesus supplies it. In the second place, *Jesus marks the direction for us*—his ideals and attitudes ought to be ours. Man has a desperate need for direction. One of his most pressing problems is "Which *way* shall I go?"

You are still asking, "How can we know the way?" In modern touring parlance we ask, "What's the direction?" All of us know that you must have directions if you are ever to arrive at your destination. Christ is a road that leads somewhere! *The Christ of the Indian Road* was a significant book title which helped to make E. Stanley Jones world-famous. Roads are not ends in themselves. They exist to get you someplace. You remember the story of the father who reprimanded his boy for spending all his money on the merry-go-round. "You have been riding all afternoon and where have you been?" John had discovered that Christ was the road, the way, to a meaningful life in which God is Father and men are brothers.

Those who believe in Christ know there is a meaning even to great turmoil and tragedy. Lord Halifax, speaking in a time of crisis in the House of Lords, told about an English country church which carries an inscription to the builder from the time, three hundred years before, when England was torn by civil war. This inscription reads: "In the year 1643, when all things sacred were either demolished or profaned, this church was built by one whose singular praise it is to have done the best things in the worst times, and to have helped them in the most calamitous." What is the way of Christ? It is a way of brotherhood, forgiveness, purity, justice, and mercy. Marjorie Farmer has caught the need for our generation:

Now, in the doorway standing;
Now, with the strange light of new sun on our faces:
The old path lost in dust; the corner sharply turned;
Standing now, timid, with loud voices,
Timid, in long words:
Lord, we beseech thee—a sign
Grant in this day of our need
The Christ before us, shining still
As when we set our backs and came this Way.[1]

The Christ way leads finally to "the place prepared for you." There is joy on the journey you will never find elsewhere. The Eternal was down among the facts when Jesus said, "I am the way."

II. Instruction—I AM THE TRUTH

Pilate asked an age-old philosophical question, "What is truth?" Philosophers from the beginning had struggled with that problem. What is the ultimate essence of things? Pilate did not wait for

[1]Prayer for the Nations, *Christian Century*, Nov. 13, 1946.

an answer from the man best qualified to give it. We moderns tend to read a philosophical answer in the phrase "I am the truth." Jesus was not a man versed in philosophy. When he said, "I am the truth," truth here corresponds with reality. God is reality and Jesus is truth because he knows God. "And the Word became flesh and dwelt among us, full of grace and truth." (John 1:14.) Truth is a living power that sets men free: Both Jesus and the Spirit are identified with the truth. Jesus is the incarnate truth. Those who have walked in his way have found his person to be true. Paul Elmer More wrote, "Oh, I understand the stupendous paradox of such a belief—who better than I?— of the belief that God, the remote and awful mystery of the world, lived and spoke and endured in the little corner of the earth called Galilee. I recite the creeds and wonder and doubt. And then I read in the Gospels, and out of some sentence or some act— out of some gesture or some glance of the eye I think it would have been had I been there to see—springs a flash of lights, comes a sudden lifting of the curtain, which compels me to say: This thing is a man and more than man."[2]

His words are true. "No man ever spoke like this man." Centuries are still re-echoing to the validity of that statement. "If your enemy is hungry, feed him." There is a categorical imperative about that statement which we cannot

[2]Quoted in: *Christian Century Pulpit*, December, 1945.

escape. Whether we feed our enemies or not, we know we ought to.

His type of life is true. Tertullian long ago said, "Truth is proved by what it produces." Mathematical truth produces an accurate balance. Chemical truth makes reactions in the test tube come out the same. The truth of physics binds the atoms together to produce an orderly universe, that does not blow up in our face until man by his perversity maneuvers atoms into a chain reaction for destructive rather than for creative purposes. Spiritual truth produces transformed lives. Christ's type of life was worth a resurrection—that is why the scriptures say, "Death no longer has dominion over him." He still produces radiant lives for those who believe on him.

Knowledge apart from ultimate truth or reality can be most dangerous. Give evil men a scientific know-how and you get a Nazi Germany. Jesus said, "Learn of me." What do we learn from him? That: God is a Father and "you are all brethren." That: God is impartially gracious to all men, "He makes his sun rise on the evil and on the good." You find the Eternal down among the facts when Jesus said, "I am the truth."

III. Provision—I AM THE LIFE

Life is that vital, vibrant consciousness of reality that gives meaning to all existence. In John's Gospel it is made plain that just as you need physical bread for physical life so you need spiritual bread for spiritual life. "My Father gives you the true bread from heaven." Jesus is "the bread which came down from heaven." He also gives the water of life of which if you drink you shall never thirst: "If any one thirst, let him come to me and drink." Just as earthly bread and water are the fundamentals for physical life, so the bread of heaven and living water are the basic essentials for the spiritual life.

In the stirring biography of Oliver Wendell Holmes, *Yankee from Olympus,* the author says of his vigorous living, "Holmes had loved life. 'If the good Lord should tell me I had only five minutes to live, I would say, "All right, Lord, but I'm sorry you can't make it ten." ' He loved life and he had believed in it. 'If I were dying my last words would be: Have faith and pursue the unknown end.' "[3] If there ever was a man who put meaning in life it was Jesus. But for him there was no unknown end. To the very last he knew that God was at the end as well as at the beginning, so all things would be well. No man lived more fully than did Jesus. How he delighted in his Father's world: "Consider the lilies of the field, how they grow . . ."

He knew the meaning of life. No humanist has ever affirmed the worth of man more positively. "Are not two sparrows sold for a penny? And not one of them will fall to the ground without

---

[3]Catherine Drinker Bowen, *Yankee From Olympus,* Little, Brown & Co., p. 416.

your Father's will." You are God's son: therefore you ought to act like His child. Those who believe on Jesus find life here and hereafter meaningful. Truly "If in this life we who are in Christ have only hope, we are of all men most to be pitied." The Eternal was down among the facts when Jesus said, "I am the life."

IV. NO ONE COMES TO THE FATHER BUT BY ME

Here we have an absolute that has struck some who have done little hard thinking, as being incongruous with all that we know of Jesus of Nazareth. Christ is not *one* way among many paths; he is the *only* road. This passage in John is not bigotry. Jesus, of all people, came to do away with prides of every kind including religious pride, the most devastating of all. But history demonstrates that his way is the only road. Only as men walk by his ideals, live by the truth of God which he incarnated, and are motivated by the same type of life which he lived—a life which included the phrase, "Do not forbid him; . . . he that is not against us is for us" —is there hope for humanity. A philosopher remarked, "That religion holds the future which shows the Eternal down among the facts." This is what St. John was saying when in his mystical way he records of Jesus, "He who has seen me has seen the Father." It means that no one can attain unto the Father except in the way—according

to the precepts, the example, and the ideals that
Jesus pointed out. The ten-year-old boy caught
this truth when he said, "Jesus was the one who
gave God a good reputation." Although some of
his followers have used the absolute, "No one comes
to the Father, but by me," in a way that would
make him shudder, when understood in the light of
his spirit it is eternally true. Robert S. Johnstone,
Jr., was killed in May, 1944, fighting the Japanese.
In his memory his parents established a scholarship at Lafayette College. Japanese applicants are
to receive priority. "Our son felt that way about
the Japanese," his father explained, adding, "We
need to understand the Christian spirit of good
will." The scholarship was financed by Robert
junior's $10,000 government insurance. The post-
war relations between the United States and the
Japanese people have proved the validity of this
act taken while passions were still hot. The parents of young Johnstone, with rare insight, demonstrated in a very practical way that the only hope
for healing the hurts of the world lies in the statement of our Lord, "I am the way, and the truth,
and the life; no one comes to the Father, but by
me."

Life's Personal Need . . .

CHAPTER THREE

Jesus Deals with Your Fear

Fear has its opposite in courage. Once there was a lad who was old enough to know what a serious operation he faced. As with little boys, and older ones too, there was the normal amount of apprehension to which he adjusted in his own boyish way. When the nurse came into the room to give him a sedative for the night he clutched some object tight in his fist and said to her, "I bet you don't know what I have in my hand!"

"No," she said. "What is it, sonny?"

"A button from the uniform of a real soldier!" The button for the lad was an emblem of the bravery soldiers ought to possess. For him it was a talisman of courage to help in overcoming the fear of the unknown.

Fear is a normal mechanism that nature has provided you. It is a great help in self-preservation. All animals from the simplest organism up to man show fear reaction under certain conditions. In fact, when animals have been bred to promote courage this can react to their own disadvantage. As an example, our family is exceedingly fond of the English bulldog—the kind with an underslung jaw, protruding teeth, and a face that only its mother

or its master can love! Through the years the Eng
lish bulldog has been bred for its courage, but interestingly enough, also in the last decades for its
gentleness. Consequently bulldogs make one of the
finest pets, for they are literally afraid of nothing
Their instinctive understanding of their ability to
meet any situation keeps them from being alarmed
at what would cause a violent reaction on the part
of smaller, less intrinsically secure dogs. Yet this
very lack of fear can be a factor of danger in the
life of the bulldog. Once we had a prize dog by the
name of Ginger. She had taken six ribbons and
was as charming in her friendliness as she was
fierce in her looks. Because of its heavy body, short
legs, and almost complete lack of nose, the English
bulldog finds it difficult to swim. Ginger did not
hesitate to jump into the water. In fact, she loved it.
She would have drowned on more than one occasion
had we not been there to bring rescue. Her lack of
fear might have been her undoing.

Fear produces either activity or paralysis. The
deer becomes frightened and immediately it bounds
off through the woods. Its fear plus its ability to
flee preserves its life. A good general knows that
being able to retreat successfully is an art every
army needs on occasion. There is some truth in
the proverb, "He who fights and runs away, lives
to fight another day." When fear produces paralysis it can help to preserve life as seen in the opos-
sum that is literally frightened into immobility. It

"plays dead" and escapes thereby. In human beings paralysis from fear is seen more often in dreams than in actual life. You may dream that a villain, animal, or a wave of the surf is pursuing you and find it impossible to move. Only fools do not fear. In Melville's classic *Moby Dick,* Starbuck, the chief mate, said that he wanted no man in his boat who was not afraid of a whale.

Fear is nearly always negative—it is a flight from the present. You never find it a pleasant experience though you may understand its biologic necessity and value. Fear is far more pervasive in man than in animals. The animal has little or no imagination, so it does not fear the non-immediate situation. Man, on the other hand, has the God-bestowed gift of imagination. You can see possible danger in many life situations in the future about which the animal has no concern at all. Cervantes in his immortal *Don Quixote* put it this way: "Fear is sharp sighted and can see things underground and much more in the skies." Man's imagination can and does become psychotic. Our age is one that has been peculiarly subject to fear because of the wars and rumors of wars, both hot and cold, that have kept all of us who have lived since 1914 in a constant state of tension.

The French philosopher Montaigne wrote, "The thing in the world that I am most afraid of is fear itself." Franklin Delano Roosevelt dramatized it for our times with his famous: "The only thing we have to fear is fear itself." There is the old and familiar story of Abraham Lincoln which bears repeating: "Two men were charging side by side in a battle. Said one, 'Why, you're pale as a sheet; you look like a ghost; I believe you're afraid.' Said the other, 'Yes, I am, and if you were half as much afraid as I am you'd have run long ago.'"

I. FEARS JESUS ALLEVIATES

In facing the problem of your fears it is well to turn to some of those incidents in the life of our Lord which show how he faced fear and help you to face it. In Matthew 14:25f, we have, "When the disciples saw him [Jesus] walking on the sea, they were terrified, saying, 'It is a ghost!' And they cried out for fear. But immediately he spoke to them, saying, 'Take heart, it is I; have no fear.'" Here we find the disciples fearful because of an illusion. Their minds had conjured up ghosts. Most of your fears of illusion will disappear if you have faith in a Christ who can conquer any situation, even to walking on the water. They really had nothing to fear, for Jesus was coming to their aid. This is not the place to discuss all of the factors connected with this incident.[1] The lesson for you here is that when Jesus really comes to you, fears vanish. They are replaced by the reality of his presence. So you can put the fears of illusion behind you if you have a great faith in Christ.

---

[1]For a full treatment see my *Preaching the Miracles of Jesus,* Abingdon-Cokesbury, pp. 72f.

You know the fear for personal safety. The continuation of this same account involves the personal safety of Peter. At heart every man wants to be a hero. When I was a boy *The Wizard of Oz* was a much-read children's book. You will remember the Cowardly Lion who was making the journey with Dorothy to the capital city so that the Wizard might give him a dose of courage which he wanted above everything else. As the story developed, the lion was courageous all along, but did not know it. Peter craved the role of the hero. After Jesus had called to the disciples and said, "Have no fear," Peter responded, "Lord, if it is you, bid me come to you on the water." Peter received permission and started on his adventure. There was no difficulty when his eyes were on Jesus, but when he began to look about and saw the tumult of the storm, he was afraid and began to sink. Lack of faith always causes people to sink. We might go on to observe that personal safety comes from Christ. Dr. Louis Warren used to say, "God's children are immortal until their work on earth is done."

You are preserved for the tasks at hand. Now Jesus does not promise you immunity from all of the ills and the dangers of life, but *he does promise his presence* to those who trust in him. After all, this is more important than personal safety. Christ was never closer to Studdert-Kennedy than in the

trenches of World War I. Jesus provided the per
sonal safety for Peter as he stretched out his han
of help. Peter was spared to learn how man
things he must suffer for his name's sake.

Many of you fear the loss of your jobs or you
livelihood. On another occasion Jesus said, "Fea
not, little flock, for it is your Father's good pleas
ure to give you the Kingdom." (Luke 12:32.) H
promised victory to his disciples in their every er
deavor. Many times during the centuries th
church has had reason to fear for the future. Th
present is one of those ages when materialism, hu
manism, communism, and a godless search for plea
ure seem so powerful. If your job in life become
an end in itself you have reason to fear, but if yo
use your position as a means to the end of buildin
God's Kingdom here on earth, you need not fea
It is said that a famous shoe manufacturer who wa
a devoted Christian had a motto especially prepare
to hang on the wall facing his desk. It read:

GOD FIRST
FAMILY SECOND
SHOES THIRD

The opposite of fear is always courage. Ameli
Earhart, first woman to fly the Atlantic, caught thi
mood:

Courage is the price that Life exacts for granting peace
The soul that knows it not

Knows no release from little things:
Knows not the livid loneliness of fear,
Nor mountain heights where bitter joy can hear
The sound of wings.[2]

All constructive work has God's blessing. Brother Lawrence testified that he felt close to God while washing the pots in the monastery kitchen. God's original command to our first parents was, "Be fruitful . . . and fill the earth." Work was to be a blessing, not a curse. There is going to be victory for God's Kingdom in heaven and *on earth* as well. This was the vision of the great Walter Rauschenbusch. It is prophetic, it is biblical, and it is true. Your job, however humble, is meaningful. Forget your fears about it and do it well, for even if you should lose it, God may have something even more significant for you.

II. FEARS JESUS ENJOINS

We have already seen that only a fool never fears. In the 12th chapter of Luke, Jesus tells us that you ought not to fear those who kill the body, but those who have power to kill the soul. After all, the Christian believes that this life is only an incident in a larger existence. During World War II, Hitler, at the height of his power, killed all of the inhabitants of Lidice, destroyed every building, and then plowed the ground on which it had been built.

[2]J. D. Morrison, *Masterpieces of Religious Verse*, Harper & Bros., Inc., p. 375.

His rage was poured out on the village because it had dared oppose his will. His purpose was to wipe it out for eternity. But the very name Lidice soon became a rallying slogan for free men everywhere. Edna St. Vincent Millay immortalized the village in a poem. After the war the citizens of the surrounding communities rebuilt the town, stick upon stick, and stone upon stone.

A false philosophy is far more dangerous than bullets. The theory of a super race dies hard. Our children were small in the days when it was still possible to get domestic help. Jiminese Brown was an attractive young Negro girl who helped my wife with the children and the chores about the home. When the time arrived for our vacation we took her with us and drove to Greenwood Lake, New York, crossing Indiana, Ohio, Pennsylvania, and into New York State. It was a revealing experience. For the first time in our lives we lived and thought somewhat as the Negro lives and thinks every day. When mealtime arrived and we stopped at a restaurant, Jiminese was not welcome. We had to take her out a plate as if she were an animal. We searched all over Washington, Pennsylvania, looking for lodging for her for one night, for Negroes were not allowed in the hotels. Some gasoline stations did not even permit her to take care of the necessities of nature. We saw with our own eyes the virus and also the stupidity of racial superiority. Our vacation journey was made wholly in northern states.

It is a twisted commentary that facilities for Jiminese would have been better had we made the journey across four southern states, but it would not
have changed one iota the curse of racial discrimination. We saw how the false philosophy of a
superior race worked with silent but deadly poison
in the midst of a free America. Jesus had said,
"Fear him who can destroy both soul and body in
hell." That part of the summer vacation was hell.
Our Lord knew of only one super race and that
was composed of those who give a cup of cold
water in his name—with all that stands for. When
you are truly a child of God you have the humility
that became Christ so majestically. "I am among
you as one who serves." (Luke 22:27.)

Those who kill the soul are the ones to fear. The
Christian needs a healthy fear of Satan and all his
works. Much of our trouble is due to the fact that
too many have felt that the Devil was a very pleasant fellow to have around occasionally. Sensuality,
alcohol, pride, selfishness, indifference—these can
and do kill and damn.

III. FEARS JESUS CREATES

St. John records the different views people had
about Jesus: "Some said, 'He is a good man,'
others said, 'No, he is leading the people astray.'
Yet for fear of the Jews no one spoke openly of
him." (John 7:12 and 13.) Jesus was a good man
who spoke divine truth, but it was not according

to the textbooks, so some thought that he was leading the people astray. Are you afraid to take his side openly on economic, social, or racial issues? It is perfectly evident where Jesus would stand, for we know that he would be against the exploitation of all unnatural advantage. In his own day the common people loved him. One of the tragedies of our age is that not all of the common people love him today. Too often they associate his church with the advantage of a privileged class. Is not one of our larger tasks to see that the common people love him in our generation as well as in his own time? Jesus was put to death because a clique feared that "he will take away our place and our nation." Jesus, his person and his doctrine, is the most dynamic and explosive force in all the world. Atom or hydrogen bombs are nothing compared to him. "His truth is marching on, glory hallelujah!" Joseph of Arimathea feared to follow Jesus openly. It was good to be a disciple; how much better it would have been to have acknowledged his discipleship.

IV. FEARS JESUS OVERCOMES

You fear sickness. Jesus could heal sickness because he destroyed the fear of sickness. The woman with the hemorrhage said to herself, "If I only touch his garment, I shall be made well." (Matt. 9:21.) She was healed by the power of God because her touch of faith showed that she no longer feared her malady would continue to plague her. Christians get sick like other folks. The difference comes in that the real Christian does not fear sickness. Hattie Barron was dying of cancer. There was no more faithful member or worker in the First Baptist Church of Malden. In all my pastoral ministry I have never seen anyone who feared cancer less than she. I finally buried her, but it was a victory, not a defeat. You fear for your loved ones even more than for yourself. Jesus helps you to overcome this terror as well. When the daughter of Jairus lay sick unto death our Lord said, "Do not fear; only believe, and she shall be well." (Luke 8:50.) Fear for your loved ones is often the most difficult of fears to overcome, but does not the Word of God teach you that God cares for your loved ones even as he cares for you? If He watches over a sparrow, how much more will He care for those near and dear to you.

If there ever was a man who knew that perfect love casteth out fear it was Jesus of Nazareth. John Macmurray has written wisely: "The immediate and necessary effect of the conquest of fear by reason is that the people in whom it is achieved find themselves trusting and loving one another. . . Human society depends on this."[3]

Finally there is the fear of death which is overcome through faith in our living Lord. The death of Jesus brought conquest over fear for Joseph of

[3]*Creative Society*, Association Press, 1936, p. 89.

Arimathea. During the life of our Lord he wa
afraid to be known as a disciple, but after the cruci
fixion he boldly asked for the body of Jesus. A
first it may seem strange that death could creat
such a transformation, but often it does. The deatl
of Florence Crittenden, beloved daughter, gave ai
entirely new interest to her wealthy father, Si
Charles Crittenden. His fortune now was a dedi
cated fortune. With it he built homes for girls al
over the world, the Florence Crittenden homes. B:
the death of an only daughter dearer to him tha:
life, he conquered the fear of death itself.

In Jesus we see the complete conquest of fea:
through faith that has been transformed by suf
fering. The only fear that our Lord ever seemec
to possess was that he might be untrue to the wil
of his heavenly Father. He knew that he had noth
ing of which to be afraid because God was with him
The same is true for you. Put your trust in th
One in whose face we see the glory of the invisibl
God. A little blind girl visiting a garden with he:
father was in an ecstasy as she went from rose t
rose inhaling their sweetness. A family frienc
came into the garden and picked her up. Normall:
timid, she showed not the slightest fear. Wonder
ingly her father asked, "Aren't you afraid? You
don't know who has you."

The child replied, "But you do, Daddy!"

John Donne's poetic beauty and genuine religiou:
insight is being rediscovered in our day. He knew
the ultimate conquest for the fear of death:

I have a sin of fear, that when I have spun
My last thread, I shall perish on the shore;
Swear by Thyself, that at my death Thy Son
Shall shine as He shines now, and heretofore;
And, having done that, Thou hast done,
I fear no more.

You may not know the outcome of all of life's situations; but you need not fear, because God knows and God cares. It was Jesus who said, "Fear not, therefore; you are of more value than many sparrows."

Life's Personal Need . . .

CHAPTER FOUR

Jesus Deals with Your Sickness

One of the most potent appeals that is possible to make to men is that of healing. All you have to do is announce a healing service in any section of the country and immediately thousands will flock to attend. Even cultured, conservative Boston saw the rise and development of Christian Science with its emphasis upon bodily healing.

I. SICKNESS, A UNIVERSAL PROBLEM

Sickness is today and has been from the beginning a universal human problem. Sooner or later you know what sickness means. It may be only the passing discomfort of seasickness, but whether rich or poor you cannot escape. Sickness is accompanied by pain and discomfort. Consequently all humanity is brought face to face with the problem of the suffering that goes along with sickness. If you are always robust in health you still face the problem because of the sickness of your loved ones or friends.

Sickness is often a revealer of fundamental human attitudes. When Job's wife saw her husband suffering with great boils she exploded bitterly,

"Curse God, and die." By contrast see the response of Job himself, "Though he slay me, yet will I trust in him" (K. J. V.). The faithful minister in his parish visits, as well as the doctor, sees both these attitudes and has to deal with them.

II. SICKNESS AND SIN

In the days of our Lord it was commonly believed that sickness or any physical disability was a direct result of sin. Thus in the case of the blind man in the 9th chapter of John's Gospel the question was asked, "Rabbi, who sinned, this man or his parents, that he was born blind?" Jesus immediately pointed out that the blindness was not caused by the sin of either the man or his parents. One problem back of the question asked our Lord was that of a healthy rascal. "The wicked flourish as the green bay tree." However, Hebrew theology did hold that ultimately the wicked would be cut down. Our own day has recognized through scientific medical understanding that there are factors that have no relation to sin which induce sickness or accidents. At the same time we need to remember that sickness is more often a by-product of sin than the modern age would like to admit. The connection between sickness and sin is seen vividly in social diseases. The biblical writer observed correctly when he wrote, "Be sure, your sin will find you out."

Some of our best Christians need to learn the

lesson that there are sins against the body that do not involve moral transgression. The terrible rise in heart disease, especially among professional men, seems to be connected with the problem of too great a work load. We break God's physical laws for our bodies and have to pay the price. Many men who are otherwise saints have grievously erred here. Mrs. Arthur Leonard was one of the godliest members of my parish in Detroit. One winter day she started on a mission of mercy to a sick neighbor. On the way she slipped on the ice, broke her hip, and after six months of long agony took up life as a cripple. Her impulse to help was good, her judgment in venturing forth was bad. It is obvious that certain types of illness are due to physical circumstances. If you have a tendency to motion sickness you have to learn to overcome it or stay home. Your physical circumstances often determine your health or lack of it. The whole theory of inoculation was discovered in Europe because it was observed that milkmaids never got smallpox. Observers noticed that these milkmaids were handling cattle that had cowpox which was evidently related to the human malady of smallpox. So men of discernment rightly saw that there must be some connection between the immunity the girls enjoyed and their employment.

III. JESUS, THE GREAT PHYSICIAN

Jesus made a very bold statement when he said of the blind man that his affliction was due neither

to his own sin nor to that of his parents. In this
he went against every accepted view of his day. He
saw clearly that sickness was not necessarily due to
sin, that other factors were involved. Yet sickness
was a terrible reality to Jesus. He saw its dire
results. To him it was not something ephemeral
conjured up by the mind. What supreme wisdom!
There is no possibility for genuine help unless you
acknowledge the reality of sickness. The appearance of any new disease immediately sends re-
search scientists and physicians on a hunt for the
cause. The Kachins of north Burma were not healed
of their various maladies until Christian mission-
aries explained to them that it was not spirits but
germs that caused disease and ill health. Typhoid
fever was endemic in our country until we realized
the necessity for an uncontaminated water supply.

There was something about our Lord that did
not allow him to tolerate sickness or any disability.
He had come to usher in God's order in which sickness ought to be as foreign as sin, for he knew that
God ultimately wills health and wholeness for His
children. "But if it is by the finger of God that I
cast out demons, then the kingdom of God has come
upon you." The leading New Testament scholar
Rudolph Otto says, "The idea of the kingship [of
Jesus] and of . . . victorious . . . miraculous author-
ity . . . was . . . this association between the kingdom
and the power which included his healing."[1]

---

[1]*Kingdom of God and Son of Man*, Zondervan, p. 55.

God surely is pleased with every effort for promoting and securing health. This is true as long as the body and its well-being does not become an end in itself. At this point health cults and those who claim a certain type of divine healing often err. Christians have had a sure instinct for the will of God and the mind of Christ as they have established and supported hospitals all over the world for the healing of the sick and the conquest of disease.

Jesus healed all who asked for healing. It was his method of philanthropy and included the morally neutral and even the unrighteous as readily as the righteous. In Jesus' healing of the ten lepers, only one had enough grace to return and thank his benefactor. The witness of his healing was in keeping with his own highest ethical teaching of God who "makes his sun rise on the evil and on the good, and sends rain on the just and on the unjust." God plays no favorites with His benevolence; neither did Jesus.

The method of Jesus' healing had to take account of the thought patterns of his day. This is seen in his use of certain mechanical means in connection with some of the incidents of healing as the mixing of clay with saliva in restoring the eyes of a blind man, or the command to "stretch out a withered hand." Jesus did not live and work in a vacuum or in the 20th century. We would expect him to think and act in terms the people of his own age could understand. This he did superbly. There are questions that have been raised about some of his methods in today's world, for we would not use an ointment of clay or saliva, but they were effective in his age. Suggestive therapy was certainly a large factor in many of his cures. He instilled confidence in the sick: "Take up your bed and go home." To-day, the wise modern physician strives to assure you that you will recover. After having pointed out that Jesus used manipulations and suggestive therapy, there is still the factor of divine power received from his heavenly Father which we cannot explain or account for. John's story (ninth chapter) of the healing of the man blind from birth is a case in point. Jesus did instill confidence. He anointed the eyes and commanded the man to do something about his own situation, "Go wash in the pool of Siloam." Yet underlying the account is the observation made, "Never since the world began has it been heard that anyone opened the eyes of a man born blind."

The Gospels are quite frank in admitting that on occasion Jesus was not able to bring about a cure. The reason for his failures is given: "He did not do many mighty works there, because of their unbelief." Here is a cue which helps to account for the ability of Jesus to heal. People who believed that the kingdom of God was at hand and that Jesus as the Messiah was proclaiming the kingdom had a mood of expectancy that made healing possible. The kingdom is one in which there will be new health as well as new words and new life. The deaf hear, the lame walk, and the blind see when the poor have the gospel preached unto them.

In our generation a minor heresy among certain Christians has arisen which contends that Christ healed then and heals today because there is healing in the atonement. In other words Christ died for sickness as well as for sin. People who hold such views are well meaning. Often they possess a faith that puts some of us to shame. At the same time they have overlooked the obvious fact that to hold to healing in the atonement cheapens the whole truth of redemption. Such a theology would make Christianity a therapeutic insurance society. The wisest and best Christians have rightly rejected it.

IV. THAT THE WORKS OF GOD SHOULD BE MANIFEST

Take the dramatic incident of the man born blind. We do not have opportunity here to go into the critical problems connected with John's Gospel, or this particular account. We simply remark in passing that the New Testament church believed that Jesus was the sort of man who could open the eyes of one born blind. There is undoubted basis in fact in this first-century conviction. We have not only an account of his healing with a theological reflection that is typical of John, but we also see how the faith and understanding of the blind man grew. To him first Jesus is a man, then he is recognized as a prophet, then he is "a man from God" and finally there is the acknowledgment of full faith: "Lord, I believe." (John 9:11-38.) The faith of the blind man grew as a result of his contacts with our Lord, so his readiness to witness also grew. In our time it is not given to all of us to be healed, just as all blind men in the land of Israel in the days of his flesh were not given sight. But, sick or well, you can have the blessedness of the presence of Christ. To paraphrase the words of Jesus in another instance: Blessed are those who have not been healed and yet have believed.

Immediately the thinking Christian asks, "Is there any value in sickness?" It means immediate discomfort, pain, and suffering. Why should this be? Possibly a partial answer is that sickness causes all men to know the meaning of pain, king and commoner alike. Saints who have suffered have long since discovered that pain can be a boon as a builder of character. The Book of Hebrews tells us that the Son of God himself was "made perfect by suffering." Those who have known severe illness and great pain often develop a kindliness and a compassion for others that they never would have possessed otherwise. A surgeon is often made a better surgeon after he has had to undergo a major operation himself.

When sickness is your portion you can turn it to the glory of God. Jesus saw clearly that neither the man born blind nor his parents had sinned "but that the works of God might be made manifest in him." You must use all of the wisdom and intelligence which God has given you to secure healing, recognizing that God has always employed natural means to heal just as he uses natural means to feed His children. God has placed on His good earth, digitalis and quinine. He has given scientists skill in manufacturing penicillin, the sulfas and antibiotics. You are not being true to Him unless you use for healing the drugs and the knowledge with which He has blessed men. God likewise gives doctors and surgeons wisdom of mind, skill of hand, and experience in practice for the healing of bodies. With it all, your ultimate faith in the healing that comes from God is enhanced rather than otherwise. Just as in the days of Jesus, you have the privilege of praying for healing and expecting an answer. Healing is from God, whether it comes through the direct hands of His Son or through the skilled hands of dedicated men and women who devote their lives to the ministry of healing. If the answer from God is not healing but, "My grace is sufficient for you," an answer given to the Apostle Paul when he prayed three times for the removal of the thorn in his flesh, then the true believer is as satisfied as was the apostle. Finally, is it not true that sometimes an illness can teach you to obey the laws of health which you were violating? And are the laws of health not the laws of God? Blaise Pascal knew this when he prayed, "I abused my health and Thou hast justly punished me for it."[2]

During my pastorate in Muncie, Indiana, one of my parishioners suffered from creeping paralysis. For fourteen years he was chained to a wheel chair. Whenever I called in the home of the elder Dwyer his cheerfulness sent me out with renewed courage. It was a humble home. Ordinarily the son would have followed in the footsteps of the father and been a laborer or a machine operator, but Vernon, by the very illness of his dad and the cheerfulness he daily witnessed, was challenged to go on and get a higher education, better preparing himself for a place of service in the community. As in the days of our Lord, the illness was an evil, but it was over-ruled "that the works of God might be made manifest."

2*World's Devotional Classics,* Vol. 6, Funk & Wagnalls, p. 183.

Life's Personal Need . . .

CHAPTER FIVE

Jesus Deals with Your Sin

Not so long ago the magazines carried pictures of two ducks submerged to their necks, frantically paddling to keep from drowning. It was an advertisement for a chemical known as a "wetting agent." The copy went on to explain that a "wetting agent" had been added to the water, soaking thoroughly the normally impervious feathers of the ducks and causing them to sink despite their best efforts. One could not help feeling sorry for the frustrated ducks that evidently could not understand what was happening to them. Sin is like a wetting agent, for sin soon has people in over their necks, often without their understanding why.

It is Jesus of Nazareth who gives buoyancy to the human spirit. Jesus stretched out a saving hand to the sinking Peter. He enables you today to counteract the sin in your life which is causing you to sink. How Jesus reacted to sin is of the utmost importance to you.

I. JESUS WAS PLAGUED BY SIN—so are you.

At the time of our Lord's birth, human selfishness, plus localized economic injustice, was such that his mother had no decent place in which to give him birth. During World War II the Archbishop of Canterbury drew up six points for a righteous new world. Each point was built around justice for the child, with the tacit understanding that if there is justice for the children there will ultimately be justice for all men.

In the person of Herod, lust to maintain a diabolical political power meant that Herod killed the babies of Bethlehem in order to try to liquidate the child Jesus. The writer of the letter to the Hebrews says that Jesus "in every respect has been tempted as we are, yet without sinning." (Hebrews 4:15.) Jesus knew what it meant to hear the siren voice of Satan. The temptations in the wilderness at the beginning of his ministry were real temptations. They can be classified as those of the body, of the mind, and of the spirit. They are typical of all that men have to undergo. Look at them for a moment. There is temptation of the body: "Turn these stones into bread; you are hungry." Of the mind: "Jump off the temple pinnacle. Mind is superior to matter. Angels will bear you up." Of the spirit: "Here are the kingdoms of the world; you can have them by doing the right thing in the wrong way." Jesus knew what temptation meant. I like the story of the humble preacher who was asked how many active church members he had. He replied, "They are all active, but they don't act right!"

Jesus was plagued by sin. The record tells us that even his own townsmen tried to throw him from a high cliff but that "passing through the midst of them he went away." Often his hearers were intolerant of his advanced but righteous moral precepts. As with all intolerant men, they simply wanted to do away with him. Finally wicked men crucified him because he answered "Yes" to the direct question, "Are you the Christ, the Son of the Blessed?" The messianic consciousness is not an easy doctrine and it presents its own problems. Yet those who have studied Jesus and walked in his way have held this to be the truest thing that could be said of him. Especially is this so when it is understood, as he unquestionably did, in the deeply spiritual overtones of a life thoroughly dedicated to doing the will of his heavenly Father.

II. JESUS HATES SIN—so must you.

Jesus hated sin as only one who knows what sin ultimately does can hate. There is a false view which pictures "blessed Jesus meek and mild." Anger and hatred can be very godly attributes. Christian discrimination comes *in knowing what to hate*. Jesus was not a social reformer in our sense of the term. To picture him as such is to take him out of his own age and place him in ours. This is a danger to which good Christians are peculiarly prone. Yet at the same time we can say that Jesus hated what we would call evil social conditions. In

speaking once of little children who had evidently
been denied the advantages that every child ought
to have, Jesus said of those who oppressed them,
"But whoever causes one of these little ones who
believe in me to sin, it would be better for him to
have a great millstone fastened round his neck and
to be drowned in the depth of the sea." (Matt. 18:6.)

Our Lord knew that lethargy toward evil is fatal.
He hated evil for what it does to men and to institutions. When Jesus saw people being gouged in
the Temple he took a whip and drove out the money-
changers. This is not the place to discuss the full
implications of this incident, but in passing we can
observe that to make Jesus a pacifist in our sense
of the term is one of those areas in which moderns
are unwarranted in reading their own concepts back
into the life of our Lord. Jesus would certainly have
had much sympathy with the modern pacifist position; but the records do not allow us to call him a
pacifist, nor on the other hand do they allow us to
put a sword in his hand. The record tells us that
he used a whip. It does not say that he hit anyone
or that he even struck an animal but certainly *he
threatened to use force if necessary* and the threat
without the intention of carrying through would
have been immortal.[1]

Mankind has slowly learned, through the events
leading up to World War II and the experience

---

[1]See my discussion in *Anglican Theological Review*, Vol. 26, p. 42;
also my *Thinking Where Jesus Thought*, Bethany Press, p. 114f.

connected with the international intervention in Korea, that sitting idly by does not save a situation. One of the most vivid pictures connected with the early Japanese invasion of China was that of a Chinese baby sitting in the middle of the ruins of a railway station, crying as if its heart would break. At the time the great nations of the earth did nothing about the violation of Chinese sovereignty, so later they had to face the full impact of Japanese militarism. On the other hand, when South Korea was invaded by the communists, democracies had learned that they must oppose evil if they were to have even a measure of peace on earth.

Sin not only wrecks nations but it also wrecks individuals. I once heard of a fellow who said that he was sure the Bible was God's Word because the only verse he had ever memorized he had discovered by personal experience to be true: "The way of the transgressor is hard"!

Jesus hated hypocrisy. Some of his bitterest invective was reserved for those who said one thing and did another, "Now you Pharisees cleanse the outside of the cup . . . but inside you are full of extortion and wickedness . . . woe to you Pharisees!" (Luke 11:39, 42.) Jesus loved men, but he did not hesitate a moment to speak against the evil they represented. One could multiply the incidents showing how Jesus hated sin and how he did something about it, while loving the sinner as the sinner has never been loved.

III. Jesus Showed COMPASSION TOWARD THE
    SINNER—so should you.

Take the incident which happened at the home
of Simon the Pharisee recorded in the seventh
chapter of St. Luke's Gospel. Jesus was having
dinner with his host. A woman of the streets whose
life had been transformed by the Master came in to
the banquet and in gratitude and contrition anointed
his feet with precious ointment and wiped them with
the hairs of her head. Simon immediately raised
a question in his mind about what was taking place.
As we read the story we expect Jesus to be courteous
to the woman whose sins, which were many, had
been forgiven. The marvelous part of the story is
that Jesus was just as courteous to Simon, whose
mental eyebrows had been raised by the incident.
Jesus answered him with the same measure of
tenderness that he showed to the woman who had
been forgiven much. He went on in just sixty-seven
words to tell a story of forgiveness that Simon
never forgot. In the story God, who was the
creditor, forgave equally freely both the large sum
and the small, and He forgave out of His abound-
ing mercy, for in the parable there is no request for
relief on the part of the debtors. To the meticulous
Pharisee the rabbi Jesus was just a casual guest;
to the woman he was her Saviour. Simon saw only
the class the woman was in (that of streetwalker);
Jesus saw her, and he sees you, as an individual
who needs saving. Simon was indifferent to such

as Mary; he could not see how self-righteously
narrow he was. The record pictures him as content to give a dinner for a visiting rabbi when
human need was crying out all around him. Did he
think his religious obligation was cared for by a
social gesture? Do you? Marguerite Wilkinson
caught his fundamental difficulty in "Guilty."

> I never cut my neighbor's throat;
>   My neighbor's gold I never stole;
> I never spoiled his house and land;
>   But God have mercy on my soul!
>
> For I am haunted night and day
>   By all the deeds I have not done;
> O unattempted loveliness!
>   O costly valor never won!

One of the most precious stories of compassion
that we possess from the life of our Lord is that
of the woman taken in adultery. It is found in some
late manuscripts of St. John's Gospel and placed
at the beginning of the eighth chapter.[2] Jesus
loathed her sin, but his ministry was one of redemption, not of condemnation. "I have not come to
call the righteous, but sinners to repentance."
(Luke 5:32.) Jesus solved the problem of sex for
this woman. He will solve it for us in the same
way: In the first place he searched her heart, in

---

[2]The intrinsic authenticity of the story is such that many present-
day New Testament scholars believe it is a genuine story of Jesus
which circulated independently and was later placed here in the
Gospel of John.

the second he was willing to forgive, and finally he put life on a spiritual basis, "Go, and do not sin again."

It is scarcely necessary to say that those who would be faithful to Christ today must show the utmost compassion toward the sinner.

IV. JESUS FORGAVE SINS—so ought you.

There are four main incidents of forgiveness which immediately come to our minds. The paralyzed man carried by four friends (Mark 2:1f); the woman who anointed his feet; the woman taken in adultery; and those who crucified Jesus, as he prayed, "Father, forgive them; for they know not what they do"![3]

Forgiveness of sins has always been at the heart of the Christian gospel. The Apostles' Creed says, "... I believe in the forgiveness of sins." Christian theology teaches that this is traceable right back to Jesus. Jesus not only forgave by his death but he also forgave by his life. Men who have loved and served him, who have honestly raised the question, "Who can forgive sin save God?" have rightly resolved this dilemma by seeing "the glory of God in the face of Jesus Christ." His type of life was so godlike that he removed the sense of guilt by his kindliness, his mercy, and his evident righteous communing with his Father. Men saw such good-

[3]The theological problem of forgiveness is discussed at length in my volume *Preaching the Miracles of Jesus,* Abingdon-Cokesbury, p. 117f.

ness in him that they felt he could impart goodness
to them as well as announce the divine forgiveness,
as did the ancient prophet Nathan (2 Sam. 12:13).
In this matter of forgiveness we need to remember
that there is divine *quid pro quo*. You must forgive
in order to be forgiven. A simple rule is to try and
not assign blame. Forgive and ask to be forgiven.
A quarrel between a husband and wife can be
resolved on such a basis. The divorce rate could
be cut in half if couples would stop trying to find
out who is at fault and ask and grant forgiveness.

Dr. Walter M. Horton in his *Our Eternal Contemporary* has a fascinating firsthand incident of a
young woman brought into a hospital who had been
stabbed in a drunken brawl in a disreputable part
of the city. She asked the nurse, "Do you think God
could forgive anyone as bad as me?" At first
frightened, the nurse, knowing the woman had only
a short while to live, replied, "I'm telling you
straight: God cares about you, and He forgives
you." The theologian commented:

> I believe that something momentous happened
> between God and that girl through that nurse,
> and that it had something to do with what hap-
> pened long ago on a certain "green hill far away
> outside a city wall." That is to say, it was
> through Christ, in His name and spirit, that the
> nurse pronounced those words of absolution. Apart
> from Christ, neither the girl's question nor the
> nurse's answer would ever have been spoken.[4]

[4]*Our Eternal Contemporary*, Harper & Brothers, Inc., pp. 83, 84.

V. JESUS CONQUERED SIN—so can you.

Sin finally crucified our Lord. F. C. Grant, a leading New Testament scholar, has well written, 'It was not the Jews, nor their rulers; it was the sin of the whole world that brought Christ to the cross. And in this view of it, we are all responsible. The whole human race share the guilt. In fact, in one sense, Christ has been slain 'from the foundation of the world.' ''[5] Death is the symbol of the conquest of sin; but death has never ruled for the Christian, for our faith is built on the resurrection. Though death is the symbol of sin's conquest, the resurrection is the glorious symbol of victory over sin. The church has rightly placed the resurrection at the very heart of its worship and its hope. We worship Christ on Sunday, the first day of the week, because this was the day on which he was raised from the dead. The high point in the Christian year is Easter which epitomizes the conquest of death and the grave by Jesus, the Lord of life. The central act of our Christian worship is the communion of the Lord's Supper. We eat the bread and drink the cup in memory of his death, but also "till he comes," which gives assurance of his present reality and his coming glory.

There is the final victory of the practical test. If you believe that Jesus conquered sin by his death on the cross, you will find victory over sins by trusting in him. Dr. Lieber of the Presbyterian

[5]Confirmed by letter.

Foreign Mission Board tells of a Chinese Christian friend who during the long conflict with Japan commanded a battalion of the simple, unlettered soldiers of China. He began a conversation about Christianity by asking them if they knew about the cross. They replied that they knew about the Red Cross. Here was the opening for which the wise Christian was waiting. Starting with the red cross of mercy on the battlefield, he told them the story of Jesus and how the black cross of sin was changed to red by the blood of our Lord.

There is more than an analogy in that story, for the Red Cross would not be so universal had it not been for the death and the resurrection of Jesus who solved the problem of sin once and for all for individuals and will solve it for nations when they start walking in his way.

Life's Personal Need . . .

CHAPTER SIX

Jesus Deals with Your Enemy

You belong to a generation raised on hate. If you are forty and older you have been conditioned three times in your life to hate rather than to forgive. First the Kaiser, then the Japanese, and now the communists. Yet all the word "kaiser" means to the younger generation is the name of an automobile! If the whipped-up attitude toward outside enemies has made you look objectively at the problem, good can come from it. But playing fast and loose with the whole idea of hating enemies can twist your soul. You get the "enemy" habit instead of the "forgiving" habit. This can mean that you must have personal enemies when you have disposed of the collective enemy. Psychologically, this could be the difficulty at the basis of the rise in our divorce rate. After World War II, we quit hating the Japanese and Germans, and started hating our wives. Instead of cultivating the blessedness of forgiveness, we nourish the cult of the trivial until it tears human relations to pieces. Some time ago, at the University of Michigan, the director of the Institute of Human Relations, of all people, was

sued for divorce by his wife, who complained that
he made an entry in a little black book every time
she burned the toast!

I. WHO IS YOUR ENEMY?

Jesus was never asked the question, "Who is my
enemy?" But he was asked the question, "Who is
my neighbor?" If any man ever lived who had
what we would call vicious and shortsighted enemies,
it was Jesus of Nazareth. Yet our Lord never
claimed that. He prayed, "Father, forgive them;
for they know not what they do." His prayers
show he considered them misinformed, rather than
vicious. The originality of Jesus is refreshing at
the point of dealing with enemies. The principal
reason for feeding our enemies, according to Jesus,
was not to heap coals of fire upon them, *but because
God loves them.* William James in commenting on
the statement of Jesus, "Love your enemies," said,
"If positive well-wishing attain so supreme a degree
of excitement, those who were swayed by it might
well seem superhuman beings . . . the effects might
conceivably transform the world."[1] Well, Jesus
did transform the world because he taught men to
forgive rather than to hate. Jesus made a genuine
advance over the Old Testament which said, "You
shall love your neighbor and hate your enemy."

[1] *Varieties of Religious Experience*, N. Y., The Modern Library,
p. 278.

God might forgive, but to the Old Testament writer, the enemy was very realistic. From the standpoint of our Lord, God had no enemies. All of those with whom he came in contact were potential children of God. Jesus' prayer, "Father, forgive them," applied to those who condemned him as well as to those who drove the nails through his quivering flesh. When Jesus said, "Love your enemies," he was talking about the individual enemy. The true test of Christianity comes in doing good to the individual, forgiving him, as Paul later put it, "as God in Christ forgave you." In his teaching about forgiving enemies, Jesus was thinking primarily about those individuals who had done wrong: the man next door whose dog digs up your flowers, the gossip in your sewing circle whose tongue is hinged at both ends. It is much easier to forgive a collective enemy than an individual one.

II. HATING YOUR ENEMY

"You have heard that it was said, 'You shall love your neighbor and hate your enemy.' " On the surface, this seems to make for integrated personality, for it means intense loyalty to one and strong opposition to the other. Something might even be said for it in a primitive society. Hate, however, is a poison which destroys the one hating as much as the one hated. In a famous statement, Booker Washington said, "You can't keep the Negro in the gutter without staying there with him." Those of us who remember the aftermath of World War I, recall how hatred of Germans persisted for years after hostilities ceased. In that unhappy land, the democratic movement was not encouraged, and all efforts to get Germany back on its feet were frowned upon. Instead of forgiving the German people for whatever part they had in participating in the war and in carrying it forward with more ruthlessness in propaganda than in fact, we persisted in hating them and our hatred backfired by the rise of Hitler, as hatred always backfires. Hatred rankles and poisons, while forgiveness blesses and heals.

At the end of hostilities in World War II the allies, instead of continuing the blockade of Germany as they had in 1918, shipped food immediately to the Germans and the Italians as well as to the French and the Dutch who had been ravished by the Nazis. America and the world learned a lesson in forgiveness with a terrible price paid by the blood of sons. By the strange economy of God, we discovered that our own best interests are wrapped up in forgiveness and helpfulness. We learned the hard way that the words of Jesus are eternally true if we are to have peace.

Hatred would never have lasted after the first world conflagration as long as it did apart from careful schooling and intense propaganda. Sometimes the children of this world are wiser than the hildren of light. One of the popular songs[2] in the mash hit *South Pacific,* which appeared after Vorld War II, goes:

> You've got to be taught to *hate* and fear;
> You've got to be taught from year to year,
> It's got to be drummed in your dear little ear,
> You've got to be carefully taught.

> You've got to be taught to be afraid
> Of people whose eyes are oddly made
> And people whose skin is a different shade,
> You've got to be carefully taught.

> You've got to be taught before it's too late,
> Before you are six or seven or eight,
> To hate all the people your relatives hate
> You've got to be carefully taught.

II. LOVING YOUR ENEMY

Treat an enemy with magnanimity and you make friend. Ulysses Grant gained the respect of Robert E. Lee and the men of the defeated South, by his courtesy, consideration, and forgiveness at Appomattox. If that spirit could have continued through the reconstruction days, our modern sectional problems would have long since faded. The great Lincoln knew this. He never hesitated to be generous and forgiving to the South or to his political enemies in the North, even when that occasioned him immediate unpopularity. Jesus taught us that we were to forgive completely—

---

[2] "Carefully Taught," Copyright, 1949, by Williamson Music, Inc. Used by permission.

seventy times seven. We were not only to forgive
we were to actively help. "If your enemy is hun
gry, feed him."

We cannot refuse action against our enemies o
God's enemies. Here is where we come into th
most difficult of Christian relations. Often, to le
an opponent have his way is the worst thing fo
him, as well as for you. Jesus did not hesita
to drive the money-changers out of the Templ
To refuse action against them would have bee
unfaithful to his highest loyalty to God. Late
he could pray asking God to forgive them, but her
he must act against their evil ways.

What, then, is Christian action against an enemy
In the first place, you must *oppose his evil inten
tions*. Almost a classic in recent years is seen i
the Berlin Airlift. The Soviet blockade of Berli
was designed to squeeze out the former allies o
Russia, and immediately force their will on th
citizens of West Berlin as well as their one-tim
allies. This was certainly evil from the standpoin
of the West. In the second place, you must *use forc
as a last resort*. Instead of punching an armore
convoy through from West Germany to Berlin wit
the very possible threat of war which this use o
force would have entailed, the United States an
Great Britain elected to establish a remarkable ai
lift which finally broke the blockade. It was a costl
process, but the total cost was far less than on
day of major warfare against the Soviet Unio

would have been. The Korean war into which the
United Nations was trapped does not vitiate this
illustration; it makes it all the more pertinent. In
the latter case, opposing evil intentions had to be
taken even at the risk of war, if that was the price
for maintaining human freedoms.

In the third place, you must *give time a chance.*
Given enough time, relations between Russia and
the West can grow bearable. Jesus underscored
this in his Parable of the Tares where he said, "Let
both grow until the harvest." In the fourth place,
you must *do your enemy active good.* A true Christian will do as Christ commands, for Christ himself
has set an example. Jesus on the cross asked his
Father to forgive those who were responsible for
his death. Do you think that prayer was heard? I
do. Jesus had said (Matt. 26:53), "Do you think
that I cannot appeal to my Father, and he will at
once send me more than twelve legions of angels?"
First Peter (2:23) says of him, "When he was
reviled, he did not revile in return; when he suffered,
he did not threaten." No wonder William James
remarked that the effects of such well-wishing to
enemies "might conceivably transform the world."
They have! It would be an interesting experiment
in real Christian action if America gave Marshall
Plan aid to Russia, but not in the spirit of the
woodshed: "This is going to hurt me more than
it does you!" We might be amazed to discover
that this type of Christian treatment of enemies,

which is certainly the type that Jesus lived and
taught, would cost us less in one year than rear
mament costs in one week.

For the average Christian the acid test for treat
ing enemies is doing active good to those who hav
lied about you or harmed you right in your own
community.

The necessity for forgiving enemies, real and
fancied, was seared on my soul early in my ministry
I baptized Thelma. She was an attractive red
headed girl who became active in the life of the
young people of the church. She even helped in
office routine. About a year after her baptism,
noticed that she stopped coming to church. In talk
ing with her, I discovered that she hated her own
sister for a fancied wrong. I said to her, "Thelma
even if she has wronged you, you must forgive
That is the very basis of our Christian faith.'
Through clenched teeth she replied, "I cannot, I
will not!" as the tears spurted to her eyes. Three
weeks later the telephone rang. We found Thelma's
lifeless body sprawled across the kitchen table with
the gas jets open.

"But I say to you that hear, Love your enemies
do good to those who hate you, bless those who curse
you, pray for those who abuse you." (Luke 6:27
28.) ". . . so that you may be sons of your Father
who is in heaven; for he makes his sun rise on the
evil and on the good, and sends rain on the just and
on the unjust." (Matt. 5:45.)

Life's Great Mysteries . . .

CHAPTER SEVEN

Your Forgiveness and Jesus

Forgiveness is one of the major problems of men and of nations. Martin Luther once said that forgiveness of sin is a knot that needs God's help to unravel. It was God in Christ who was best able to untie the knot of sin that had bound men so tightly. More than any among the sons of men Jesus forever proved that forgiveness does work.

Those in the Church of Jesus Christ who have learned from him the approach to the problem of forgiveness have found a solution for one of the most vexing and perennial difficulties men have to face. Some time back I came across a fascinating instance of forgiveness. Here it is: Years ago, in Winchester, Virginia, there was a boy by the name of Charles Broadway Rousse, the son of a poor working woman and a dead father. He went to Sunday school, sang in the choir, and was a useful member in that little church of poor and inconspicuous people. By and by the boy fell in with evil associates, was implicated in a crime, and was sent to the penitentiary. After a bit the members of the church got up a petition to the governor and had the boy pardoned. They sent a delegation and brought him home. On their arrival home, they went

71

directly to the little church where all the congregation had gathered, and there in the presence of all the people exercised the divine function that has been committed unto the church: they forgave his sins. They said to him, "We want you to come right back into the church and take your place in the Sunday school and the choir. The past is blotted out, *forgiven and forgotten,* and is as though it had never been." Then, one by one, all the members of the church took him by the hand, personally ratifying the action of the church, and expressing their confidence.[1]

I. GOD FORGIVES

In thinking about the approach of Jesus to this problem we instinctively turn to the major incidents in his life in which he demonstrated what he had taught about forgiveness when he said, on the cross, "Father, forgive them; for they know not what they do." Here Jesus assumes that God is forgiving. *"Father,* forgive." The type of forgiveness which takes the highest spiritual understanding is for a parent to forgive those who have wilfully wronged his child. Presumably as the nails are driven, there is wrung from the lips of our Lord this anguished prayer. Jesus believed that his heavenly Father would forgive even under these circumstances.

----

[1]Edgar DeWitt Jones's column, *Detroit Daily News,* Jan. 12, 1944.

Now, back of forgiveness is the need for it. You sin against your neighbor, you sin against God. A generation ago a naïve theology laid little emphasis upon sin or the need for forgiveness. A. C. McGiffert, a liberal of the Ritschlian school, held that to conceive of the gospel in terms of divine forgiveness is a misunderstanding. "What is really needed by a sinner is not forgiveness. He should be educated away from that idea; and we should be, too. The sinner needs moral impulse and power."[2] Little Jane, who had just learned to read, knew better. One day with her mother she visited an old burying ground. Both mother and daughter were reading the epitaphs. Suddenly, Jane stopped and said, "Mother, don't they ever bury sinners?" We have not lived through two world wars, a depression, a cold war, a warm war, and general sinful devilment, for nothing. Our generation knows that men are sinners. Modern theology, like biblical theology and our daily paper, underscores that what this world needs most is forgiveness. God's forgiveness is proof of a moral universe. In the material world God's laws are unchanging. If this were not so, Whirl would be King. A universe with its orderliness would have been impossible. The Christian theist believes that God made physical laws unchangeable. One winter recently in New England it snowed every single Sunday for three solid months, not because God had it in for the

[2]*Christianity as History and Faith,* Charles Scribner's Sons, pp. 203, 207.

church, but because He allowed His laws to operate. Christian character is built when you go *through the snow to church.*

> It's a mile and a half from church, you know,
> And it snows today, so we just can't go.
> We'd go ten miles to a dance or show
> Though the rain should fall and the wind
>   should blow,
> But the church is different, we'd have you know.

Moral law, apart from grace, is as unchangeable as physical law. "The wages of sin is death." But if there is forgiveness, then you know that you do not live in an inexorable universe. Forgiveness is the best proof of God's personal character. In Jesus' Parable of the Prodigal, the father gladly forgave his son, so Jesus taught that God gladly forgives us. "Redemption is God's way of being moral."[3] E. P. Dickie has said: "The thought of Divine pardon is not unethical, but beyond ethics."[4]

> There's a wideness in God's mercy,
> Like the wideness of the sea.

II. YOU MUST FORGIVE

You can be a part of the physical universe without forgiving. They say an elephant never forgets an injury. But you cannot be a part of the moral universe without forgiving. Jesus said, "God is love." You can forgive without loving. You can-

---

[3] J. S. Whale, *Christian Doctrine*, Macmillan Co., p. 77.

[4] *Rev. & Response*, Charles Scribner's Sons, p. 262.

not love without forgiving. Here is a major Christian axiom: If you want to be a child of God, then you must forgive.

At the heart of the Lord's Prayer is the assumption of a forgiving spirit on the part of believers: "And forgive us our debts, as we also have forgiven our debtors." (Matt. 6:12.)

Why must you practice forgiveness? Because in the spiritual realm if you receive it and do not practice it, this becomes a positive incentive for further wickedness on your part. In the Parable of the Unmerciful Servant: "The big debtor had not troubled about the little debt due to him, knowing that whatever came to him belonged to his creditor, but when his debt was forgiven, whatever he could squeeze out of the little debtor became his own. The forgiveness which he had received, not moving his spirit in like kind, became a positive incentive in the opposite direction."[5]

III. FORGIVENESS A PREREQUISITE TO FORGIVENESS

The necessity for forgiveness is an emphatic teaching of Jesus. There is a divine *quid pro quo* —this for that. Here are a few of the statements of our Lord about forgiveness:

Matt. 6:12—"And forgive us our debts, as we also have forgiven our debtors."

---

[5] A. T. Cadoux, *Parables of Jesus*, London, J. Clarke and Co., Ltd., p. 214f.

Matt. 6:14—"For if you forgive men their trespasses, your heavenly Father also will forgive you."

Matt. 6:15—"But if you do not forgive men their trespasses, neither will your Father forgive your trespasses."

Matt. 18:35—"So also my heavenly Father will do to every one of you, if you do not forgive your brother from your heart."

Mark 11:25—"And whenever you stand praying, forgive, if you have anything against any one; so that your Father also who is in heaven may forgive you your trespasses."

Luke 6:37—". . . forgive, and you will be forgiven."

What our Lord is stressing here is that forgiveness cannot penetrate your heart until you forgive. Forgiveness is just as essential to the preservation of the moral universe as the law of gravity is to the preservation of the physical universe. Here "we touch what is one of the most remarkable points in the teaching of Jesus. . . He who would be forgiven must himself forgive."[6]

IV. FORGIVENESS MUST BE INFINITE

On one occasion Peter came to Jesus with a problem about forgiveness, saying, "Lord, how often shall my brother sin against me, and I forgive him? As many as seven times?" Jesus said to him, "I do not say to you seven times, but seventy times seven." (Matt. 18:21, 22.) Peter is here typical

[6]T. W. Manson, *The Teaching of Jesus*, Cambridge University Press, p. 311.

of our small legalisms. It is quite likely that Jesus in his response had in mind Gen. 4:24:

> "If Cain is avenged sevenfold,
> Truly Lamech seventy-sevenfold."

As in olden days there was no limit to hatred, so in the time of the kingdom which our Lord came to establish there would be no limit to forgiveness.

You must forgive seventy times seven. Have you ever stopped to think what chance you would have if God grew weary of forgiving you? In asking the question Peter was likely thinking about the rabbinic position which held that you ought to forgive three times, going back to Amos 2:6. In his own mind he was generous: Christian legalism ought to be more than twice as considerate as Jewish legalism! No so with Jesus. He delighted in the opportunity of stressing the *unlimited* beneficence of God, his Father and ours. There could be no legalism in his kingdom. Mercy and forgiveness must always be on the highest plane. That is a gospel that has gone shouting down the centuries.

V. JESUS PRACTICED FORGIVENESS

Our Lord prayed for his tormentors. If he had come down from the cross as his enemies suggested they would not have believed, they would simply have feared. We have his word for it that they would not believe if one rose from the dead. While his enemies badgered him, Jesus prayed for them, "Father, forgive them; for they know not what they do." That is far more than a prayer for the rough soldiers who are carrying out orders. It is for the hard legalists of his day—and ours—for Caiaphas, Pilate, and all of us whose sins helped nail him there.

At the conclusion of John's Gospel is a beautiful story about the restoration of Simon Peter to favor with Jesus. Peter had denied him. He was a traitor. Jesus had every human right to read Peter out of the party. Jesus not only forgave, *he restored,* which is what you must do. In this incident, as well as by his whole life, Jesus taught that forgiveness is not simply saying the words, it is *restoring to favor and place.* So Peter today for half of Christendom is the head of the church; and for all of us Peter and Paul are considered the two chief apostles. You can see what Jesus did for him when he forgave him!

Those who follow Jesus must practice forgiveness. "A servant is not greater than his master." An excellent Christian exercise is to look up someone who has wronged you and forgive him, *being sure to restore him to the place and station he once held.* If you have accepted forgiveness at God's hands, you must grant forgiveness, because *this is the only way to maintain harmony in the moral universe.*

One of Reinhold Niebuhr's finest insights is that the consciousness of being forgiven following a realistic facing of one's own sin, is the one thing that prevents self-righteousness. On it, you can build a solid life. Does it work? Let us go back to Charles Rousse: Not long after, the boy's genius awoke. He went to New York City and became one of the greatest business princes in America, but, as Dr. Jones tells it, "he could never forget the people who had forgiven and saved him. He showed kindness to the children of those who had forgiven him. He gave to the city a water, light and sewerage system, gave a beautiful cemetery, a great free library, and benefactions of every kind. On the spot where that little church stood, he erected one of the most beautiful churches on this continent, and over the threshold he had carved these words, 'To the Divine Love that lives in the heart of men.' "[7] Charles Rousse learned the true meaning of forgiveness from the Master of men, who taught us that God forgives in us far more than we will ever have to forgive in others.

---

[7]Edgar DeWitt Jones, *op. cit.*

Life's Great Mysteries . . .

CHAPTER EIGHT

Your Suffering and Jesus

One of the great preachers of Great Britain is John Arthur Gossip. Over a quarter of a century ago his wife died. The next Sunday, Gossip was in his pulpit as was his custom. His topic has become world-famous: "But When Life Tumbles In, What Then?" He closed one of the most moving sermons of our generation with these words, "No, not death. For, standing in the roaring of the Jordan, cold to the heart with its dreadful chill, and very conscious of the terror of its rushing, I too, like Hopeful, can call back to you who one day in your turn will have to cross it, 'Be of good cheer, my brother, for I feel the bottom, and it is sound.' "

Not long after this Dr. Gossip published a volume of sermons. It was dedicated: "To my wife, my constant companion still." Nearly twenty years later he published another volume of sermons with this dedication of poignant beauty, "To my wife, now a long time in the Father's house." The first dedication is what we might expect, the second is evidence that even the world-famous preacher had carried through the years a burden of loneliness of which others were not aware. The problem of suf-

fering is as old as the human race. There is no
home but that finally knows it. I can remember my
preacher father, John Roach Straton, saying,
"There is an old Spanish proverb which goes,
'There is no home without its hush.' "

I. JESUS KNEW SUFFERING

Like all other men Jesus knew suffering. We believe that he was and is the Son of God, but orthodox Christian theology holds that he was likewise
son of man. The first major heresy in the Christian
church is known as Docetism; New Testament pas-
sages were written especially to combat it. This
view taught that Jesus did not really suffer, that
he was a God who could not suffer, he only appeared
to suffer on the cross. As a sensitive soul we would
expect Jesus to suffer. He did. He knew physical
homelessness, "The Son of man has nowhere to
lay his head" yet Jesus never let personal physical
need interfere with his message. He suffered at
the sight and the thought of evil. There is every
evidence that evil situations gave him intense pain.
Scholem Asch has vividly portrayed this in his
novel, *The Nazarene,* where he has drawn upon his
imagination to picture Jesus indignant as he viewed
the sweat-shop conditions of the dye and woolen
factories of ancient Tyre. With true insight the
novelist has seen how Jesus would rebel against all
exploitation. Jesus knew the suffering attendant
upon the rejection of his message. Almost wistfully

he asks the disciples, "Will you also go away?"
Then we see unrestrained sorrow at the grave of
his friend Lazarus when the record tells us, "Jesus
wept."

There is no suffering or pain apart from sensitiveness. No sensitiveness means no life. Steak
in the frying pan does not suffer. Because Jesus
was the highest embodiment of life, he had a supreme sensitiveness. His suffering would be peculiarly acute. There was a new factor in his own
faith which he faced. As his message was rejected
and it became increasingly evident that the religious
leaders of his day would have none of him, Jesus
realized that he would have to pay the price of
their rejection, that he would have to suffer.

II. THE SUFFERING SERVANT

Jesus was intimately familiar with the prophecy
of Isaiah, having quoted it on more than one occasion. In Isaiah 53, whether the Suffering Servant
is thought of as the people Israel or whether it is
epitomized by an individual person (and both
thoughts are in the passage), Jesus surely had pon-
dered long upon its message of redemptive suffering. To the best of our knowledge Isaiah 53 was
not considered messianic in the time of Jesus, yet it
unquestionably had a bearing upon our Lord's own
conception. That the church soon interpreted this
passage messianically was due to the suffering of
Jesus on the cross, plus his own divine insight into

the ultimate nature of his ministry. "The Son of man must suffer many things, and be rejected . . . and be killed" (Mark 8:31). Until the time of Jesus, the Messiah, the anointed, was thought of as a conqueror, a ruler, a reformer, who was coming on the clouds of heaven or out of the sea. He was one whose "winnowing fork is in his hand" (Matt. 3:12).

The author of Hebrews with deep Christian insight says that Jesus was "made perfect by suffering." In the famous Caesarea Philippi experience where Jesus asked the disciples, "Who do you say that I am?" and Peter replied, "You are the Christ," Jesus went on to say that as the Messiah he must go up to Jerusalem and suffer many things, be killed, and be raised again the third day. In the light of the resurrection fact, the phrase, "be raised again the third day," carries a weight with us that it did not with those who first heard it on the lips of our Lord. What they heard was that he must suffer; at the time of its utterance his final victory was an undertone.

It was an idea immediately rejected by Peter and doubtless by the other disciples as well. "God forbid, Lord! This shall never happen to you!" Almost with vehemence Jesus turned on him and said, "Get behind me, Satan! For you are not on the side of God, but of men." We can paraphrase: "You haven't the faintest understanding of how God looks at life." Suffering was a part of the providence of God and even the Messiah was not to be spared.

The best reason in the world to consider that Jesus was the Messiah, the anointed of God, is that he had a passion to do God's will at whatever cost. He put a deeply spiritual content into the term. His suffering was one that was voluntarily assumed. The record tells us: "He set his face to go to Jerusalem" and "I lay down my life. . . . No one takes it from me." The picture of the crucifixion that has made the most profound impression upon me was not painted by one of the Great Masters. It does not show Jesus writhing in agony on the cross, rather it pictures our Lord standing by the cross with his eyes uplifted. The time is just before the rough soldiers take him and stretch his living body on the piece of wood. In the Master's face is evidence that God was with him in this moment when his sensitive soul must have suffered far more in the anticipation of the agony than when the actual nails were thudding through his flesh.

Christian theology uses the word "vicarious" in connection with the suffering of Jesus. It has been a sure insight, for he did suffer for us, you and me, the just for the unjust. Even Pilate asked the question, "Why, what evil has he done?" Luke says that suffering was a part of the divine plan, "Thus it is written, that the Christ should suffer. . . ." (Luke 24:46.) The author of Hebrews ties together the suffering with the redemption. He became "a merciful and faithful high priest in the service of God, to make expiation for the sins of the people.

For because he himself has suffered and been tempted, he is able to help those who are tempted.'' (Hebrews 2:17, 18.) Most of us pay the penalty for our own sin or carelessness. When you disregard the laws of physics and stumble with a glass vase in your hands, you can give yourselves a nasty gash. The prophet Habakkuk struggled with the suffering of his people at the hands of the wicked Babylonians: While the men of Israel were far from perfect, they were angels compared to the Babylonians. Yet God in His infinite wisdom sometimes uses the wicked to punish those who are far more virtuous than they. But with our Lord it was a case of spotless purity suffering gladly that men might be redeemed. Jesus had taught, ''Unless a grain of wheat falls into the earth and dies, it remains alone; but if it dies, it bears much fruit.'' (John 12:24.) Jesus not only believed this for others, he believed it for himself. His faith has been rewarded by those who have assurance that he provides redemption for them. You can have many theories about what took place on the cross. The practical fact remains that faith in Jesus has the power to ''change a radically bad man into a radically good man.''

III. THINGS THAT BE OF GOD

If you believe in God and trust in Christ you must suffer. What a strange doctrine! Rather it would seem that you should become a cosmic pet because of your belief and obedience. Yet the greatest of the prophets have known that suffering was somehow a part of the providence and wisdom of God. At times Jeremiah almost railed at God because of suffering, "Why is my pain unceasing, my wound incurable, refusing to be healed? Wilt thou be unto me as a liar, like waters that fail?" (Jer. 15:18 K.J.V.) Calling God a liar; imagine that! God did not drive Jeremiah off because of his brashness; He drew him closer, and the prophet through faith could recognize the hand of God in his travail. Jesus places self-denial, cross-bearing and suffering as central for those who would follow him.

Suffering and trial does develop the noblest qualities. What hours do we remember with greatest pride in America? They are 1776, 1863, 1917, and the holocaust of Pearl Harbor in 1941. In the future we will not take pride in the roaring twenties but the dangerous forties and challenging fifties. Trial and temptation overcome gives double strength. Guido Reni has a picture in the Louvre which shows Michael with his foot on Satan's throat. William James in a well-remembered comment on it said, "The world is all the richer for having a devil in it, so long as we keep our foot upon his neck!"

In the strange economy of God, strength does come through suffering. John Bennett remarks, "Without suffering life is lived on a superficial level; we become self-sufficient, complacent, and proud. Suffering deepens and strengthens every quality which we have. It can purify us from pre-occupation with trivial things. It raises love and comradeship to the highest level. It forces us out of ruts and often gives life a new beginning."[1] No public figure in the past century suffered more or faced it more bravely than did Robert Louis Steven-son. Hear him:

To go on forever and fail and go on again,
And be mauled to the earth and arise,
And contend for the shade of a word, and a thing not seen
    with the eyes,
With the half of a broken hope for a pillow at night,
That somehow the right is the right,
And the smooth shall bloom from the rough. . .[2]

Prior to World War II a major contribution to that tragedy was a statement signed by 11,000,000 people in Great Britain that under no circumstances would they go to war again. This made Hitler bold in planning his depredations. During this period Chamberlain returned from Munich waving the ca-pitulation to Hitler as he announced that it would bring "peace in our time." By contrast see how the whole world was stirred with the words of Win-ston Churchill, "If England shall last for a thou-sand years it will be said, this was her finest hour.... We shall draw from the heart of suffering itself the means of inspiration and survival." Strange though it seems, blessing comes through suffering.

---

[1]*Christian Realism*, Charles Scribner's Sons, p. 179.
[2]"If This Were Faith," *Poems & Ballads*, Charles Scribner's Sons, 1913, p. 227.

Some time ago the President of the University of Florida, who apparently had every evidence of wealth and position in life, was accused, by a person who did not know of his background, of being born with a silver spoon in his mouth. Here was his reply: "In a neighboring state some years ago there was a woman who had been deserted by her husband and who was laboring in a cotton mill in order to buy a crust for her three children. One day she dragged herself to work, though anyone could see that in her condition she would be better off in the hospital. But the picture of her hungry children drove her on. In the middle of the morning, she had to leave the looms and was carried into a bare and cold adjoining room where, attended only by two of her fellow-workers, she gave birth to a boy. That boy, gentlemen, happened to be me." The suffering and sacrifice of his mother had been a challenge to the great educator all of his life. It is entirely possible that the circumstances of his birth in a stable in Bethlehem helped to give inspiration to our Lord in his ministry to the poor as he preached the gospel unto them.

Jesus taught us fully by his own life that knowledge of God comes through suffering. Out of the agony of the Garden of Gethsemane came even a greater understanding of the will of his heavenly Father. "If it be possible, let this cup pass from me; nevertheless, not as I will, but as thou wilt.' Kierkegaard once said, "The bird on the branch the lily in the meadow, the stag in the forest, the fish in the sea, and countless joyful people sing— God is love! But under all these sopranos, as it were a sustained bass part, sounds the *de profundis* of the sacrificed: God is love.''[3]

Finally on the cross Jesus demonstrated the complete knowledge of and faith in God: ''Father, into thy hands I commit my spirit!'' He knew God was with him in the suffering of the cross. We, too, know that God was with him for we see it in the events connected with his life, his death, and his glorious resurrection. We see it in the history of his church through the centuries. We see it most of all in the lives of those who are changed by faith in him.

IV. SUFFERING THAT IS REDEMPTIVE

In all probability, you have seen in your own life how involuntary suffering when it is rightly faced can and does bring strength and a blessing. It is true as you watch others. It is true when you suffer yourself. Most of our suffering and pain is in this category. If involuntary suffering strengthens character, how much greater does suffering that is *voluntarily assumed* bring redemption. Especially is this so when it is suffering consciously incurred for others.

[3]*The Journals* quoted in *Kierkegaard Anthology*, Princeton University Press, 1927, p. 26.

Have you heard the story of Arthur St. Germaine? During World War II, "He submitted himself to a serum experiment conducted by Navy researchers seeking to shield soldiers, sailors, and marines from death by disease. Thirty-nine others no less courageous took the same chance. So far, young St. Germaine has been the only one of the Massachusetts prison group to give his life in the experiment, but there is a debt to them all. The man who lays down his life that others may live atones for most of the crimes that man in his frailty is tempted to commit. That Gov. Leverett Saltonstall granted Arthur St. Germaine a posthumous pardon is mere symbolism. He had washed his record white in his manner of dying." So wrote the *Detroit Free Press*, December 4, 1942, as it gave the account prominent space on its editorial page under the title "Greater Love Hath No Man." From a Christian standpoint the editor's theology may be fuzzy but there is still a catch to the throat and a challenge to the heart in such a story. If the inmate of a penitentary could move men to greater sacrifice by his own life and death, *how much more* can the Son of God transform those who put their faith in him by his death on Calvary! Early Christians with genuine insight saw Isaiah 53 as a foregleam of what Christ has done for mankind. "Surely he has borne our griefs and carried our sorrows; yet we esteemed him stricken, smitten by God, and afflicted."

"A few hours of endeavor and endurance on the rack of the cross have an absolute value that will last when all our works are obliterated like scratching on the sand," somewhere wrote Father Tyrrell. Jesus faced the problem of suffering for himself. Jesus triumphed over death and the grave by absolute faith in the ultimate goodness of God. For those who put their trust in Christ there is the same triumph.

Life's Great Mysteries . . .

CHAPTER NINE

Your Death and Jesus

No study of the problems which Jesus helps to solve is complete without treating the major problem, that of your death. Beside this overwhelming fact all other problems fade into insignificance. Most of us are ready with Browning to say:

I would hate that death bandaged my eyes, and forebore
    And bade me creep past.
No! Let me taste the whole of it. . .

It is soon past and you will take what the next world has in store for you with a modicum of courage. But when death pounces on one dearer than your own being, what then? Does Jesus have anything to say to you? Does faith in him make any difference? Back of this question is a startling discovery in my own ministry.

In a quarter of a century of preaching, I found that I had never preached a sermon on death. There have been many sermons on life, on immortality, on the resurrection, on heaven. There have even been a few on hell, as part of the whole teaching of the Bible, but there was not one on death. Of course, death has been mentioned in many of the other messages, but it was never treated specifically. Yet, if there is an afterlife, its portals are the gates of death.

I. DEATH IN THE BIBLE

In most of the Old Testament, death is thought of as final. It was not until late in the development of Hebrew religion that an afterlife began to be considered as an aftermath of death. Ecclesiastes underscores the universality of death, "What befalls the fool will befall me also." There is an inevitability about it, "For of the wise man as of the fool there is no enduring remembrance." There was little hope for the author of Ecclesiastes or for the Psalmist who said, "For in death there is no remembrance of thee; in Sheol who can give thee praise?" The Hebrew thought largely of service for God in the present life. Continuation of existence for many Old Testament writers was in terms of the family and the projection of one's personality through one's children.

By the time of Jesus a definite belief in the resurrection had developed in Jewish thought. It is the New Testament, however, that sings a paean of praise to God for the gift of eternal life through Jesus Christ, our Lord: "O death, where is thy victory? O death, where is thy sting? . . . thanks be to God, who gives us the victory through our Lord Jesus Christ." In the New Testament, death is still inevitable, Heb. 9:27: "It is appointed for

men to die once, and after that comes judgment."
Yet in this verse death is clearly not the end. For
better or for worse, there is judgment. There is
something that follows: Briefly the New Testament
teaches that the world is under the reign of death
(Rom. 5:17). There is a sting to it and a victory
to the grave (1 Cor. 15:55). It is the eternal enemy
of man that shall at last be destroyed (1 Cor. 15:26).
However, the real terror is not in physical death,
but in the final loss of all spiritual hope which the
New Testament terms "the second death" (Rev.
20:14). Paul had no fear of physical death, or the
original fear was so transformed by his faith in
the resurrection of Jesus, that he could calmly
state that he felt that it would be better to depart
because he would be present with the Lord (2 Cor.
5:6-8). Early Christians faced death triumphantly.
Their faith taught that because Christ lives, they
too would live. Vital Christianity has had similar
faith from that day to this.

Back of the New Testament faith lies the life,
teachings, death, and resurrection of our Lord.
Jesus had little to say about death or life after
death, far less than Paul. He was living this life
too fully to be overly concerned about the next. For
him the other world had a reality it is difficult for
us to comprehend today.

The realm and reign of his Father was as obvious
as the sunrise. Once we hear him say under stress,

"Do you think that I cannot appeal to my Father, and he will at once send me more than twelve legions of angels?" (Matt. 26:53.) These legions were far more to him a part of God's world than feeble Roman cohorts or bands of Temple guards.

II. FAITH IN THE RESURRECTION

Along with the Pharisees, Jesus believed in a resurrection. It was he who gave them the answer to the catch question of the Sadducees about seven brothers who had married in succession one woman; with smugness they had asked, "Whose wife shall she be in the resurrection?" Our Lord replied, "In the resurrection they neither marry nor are given in marriage, but are like the angels in heaven. And as for the resurrection of the dead, have you not read what was said to you by God, I am the God of Abraham, and the God of Isaac, and the God of Jacob'? He is not the God of the dead, but of the living." (Matt. 22:30-33.)

As with devout Pharisees, Jesus thought of the next life as sitting with Abraham or being in Abraham's bosom: ". . . many will come from east and west and sit at table with Abraham, Isaac and Jacob in the kingdom of heaven" (Matt. 8:11). The eschatological note is evident in a number of parables. We see it in the householder who shut his door (Luke 13:25f.): ". . . you will weep and gnash your teeth, when you see Abraham and Isaac and Jacob and all the prophets in the kingdom of

God and you yourselves thrust out." Again it is
evident in the story of the rich man and Lazarus
(Luke 16:19ff). The rich man appeals to father
Abraham, they carry on an intelligent conversation
but there is a great gulf fixed between the place of
Lazarus and that of the selfish man of wealth.

An unmistakable part of the tradition of the
teachings of Jesus is bound up with the matter of
his rising again after three days. We get it first
at the Caesarea Philippi experience, ". . . the Son
of man must suffer many things . . . and be killed
and after three days rise again" (Mark 8:31).
Peter did not understand at the time and there
have been many who have been puzzled since. At
one of the visits to Jerusalem at the Passover festi-
val, John tells us that Jesus in bitter controversy
with his opponents said, "Destroy this temple and
in three days I will raise it up. . . . But he spoke
of the temple of his body" (John 2:19-21). His
enemies used this statement with telling effect at
his trial. "We heard him say, 'I will destroy this
temple made with hands, and in three days I will
build another, not made with hands'" (Mark 14:58;
also: 15:29; Matt. 27:63). There is an echo of it
also in Acts 6:14 in the speech of Stephen. The
record is clear that Jesus believed that in some way
he would return after three days. It is possible
that Jesus was influenced by the Enoch literature
(Enoch 71:14) in which it is finally disclosed to
Enoch that Enoch himself was the son of man.

Jesus may have thought that, like Enoch, he would become the son of man at the time of his return "after three days." In any event death held no terror for Jesus.

It is to John's Gospel that we must turn for the clearest statement about what happens after death "in my Father's house." Here in that sacred and mystical last discourse with his followers Jesus comforts his distressed disciples: "In my Father's house are many rooms; if it were not so, would I have told you that I go to prepare a place for you? .. that where I am there you may be also" (John 14:2-3).[1] Jesus sees the other life as one in which there is an opportunity to continue God's work. He was to be active preparing a place for his followers and he wanted them to be with him.

However, it is in the transforming fact of the resurrection that Jesus taught most powerfully about victory over death. It was a deed rather than a word; "See my hands and my feet, that it is I myself; handle me, and see; for a spirit has not flesh and bones as you see that I have." (Luke 24: 39.) The New Testament faith is built on the New Testament fact that Jesus is not dead but alive.

---

[1]There is no point here in going into the large controversy over the Johannine literature and whether we have in the Gospel the *psissima verba* of Jesus. Suffice it to say that the older critical view that John is to be completely discounted is no longer valid. Some of the most interesting New Testament investigation is now being done in this Gospel and much of it supports more traditional views.

III. YOU AND YOUR DEATH

For you death is something that happens to the other fellow. You build a stoical philosophy about it. Perhaps this is a beneficent escape mechanism which enables you to live in the midst of death without having the thought of it drive you mad. Although death is something that happens to the other man and the other family, it finally happens to you and to yours. You can never know its total poignancy until it comes into your own immediate circle. Modern man, for all of his vaunted advance cannot flee death. Some time ago Dean Willard Sperry, at the death of a famous Harvard scholar said, "The academic mind resents being reminded of the fact of death." We may lay bare the heart of the atom, search out the borders of the universe even in time discover the mystery of life, itself, but death will still remain the nemesis of the secular mind.

O weariness of men who turn from GOD
To the grandeur of your mind and the glory of your action,
To arts and inventions and daring enterprises,
To schemes of human greatness thoroughly discredited, . .

Though you forget the way to the Temple,
There is one who remembers the way to your door:
Life you may evade, but Death you shall not.
You shall not deny the Stranger.[2]

---

[2]From *The Rock*, by T. S. Eliot, copyright, 1934, by Harcourt Brace, and Company, Inc.

There is a fear of death. You simply must face it, for yourself and your family. Browning's situation made him braver than most of us:

> Fear death?—to feel the fog in my throat,
> The mist in my face, . . .
> No! let me taste the whole of it. . .

But Elizabeth Barrett, his wife, was dead. He would have feared death more if she had been living. You fear death because death means the *unknown*. There is always a shrinking from what you do not know.

When attending the first session of the World Council of Churches at Amsterdam, Mrs. Straton and I landed at Cherbourg. All of the other passengers took the boat train to Paris, but at that time we did not wish to go to Paris. We wanted to go to Mont St. Michel, ninety miles south of Cherbourg. On the boat we could secure no information about train or bus schedules to this famous monastery built off the coast of France, one of the wonders of the world. Our French was rusty; the customs were new and strange, so there was a bit of fear and timidity in striking out on one's own in a foreign country. Even though I had been a seagoing radio operator during my college days and had been in many exotic lands, here was a new experience traveling with a wife. Yet in many ways this turned out to be the most interesting part of the whole trip. The people of France were the soul of courtesy and helpfulness. So the adventure that seemed somewhat of an ordeal before it began developed into one of the most delightful experiences we have had together. "For now we see in a mirror dimly." Heaven, for all of its streets of gold and gates of pearl, is a very generalized place. We are not familiar with it, and the very fact of the unknown makes us shrink. Even though the Bible depicts heaven in such glorious terms we know that it also speaks of hell. Whatever the latter is like, it is not a place to be sought. For Jesus, God's reign and God's care for even the sparrow were so obvious that you might say there was no unknown.

Death means *separation*. Man is a gregarious creature. You do not like separation from those you know and love. You avoid it at every opportunity. Consequently, you fear the earthly separation of death. There was no separation for Paul—it was "absent in the body and present with the Lord." There was no separation for Jesus—it was, "Father, into thy hands I commit my spirit!"

Death also means *Finality*. Its irrevocable character, its finality, its complete leaving of all that you know and love, is one of the most terrifying things about it. It comes alike to the great as well as the little of this earth—"what befalls the fool will befall me also."

IV. WHY DEATH?

When you ask the question, "Why must there be death?" you need to remember that the plans of

God are good, "and God saw everything that he
had made, and behold, it was very good." Life is
the supreme achievement in God's plan. A rose, a
horse, a man—anything that lives—is more wonderful than a whole galaxy of stars that simply burn.
Yet for life to be possible with all of its worth, death
had to be.

In fact, the necessity for death was born the
moment life was created. "You are dust, and to
dust you shall return." Now, if life is good, and
we believe that it is, then *death also must be good*.
The biologist tells us of a nitrogen cycle which con-
tinues to make life on earth possible. It is the death
of plants and animals that gives life in turn to other
plants and animals.

Did you ever consider that Adam and Eve had to
die in order to make a place for you and for me?
Aeons ago a "Standing Room Only" sign would
have been hung on earth. The lift of human love
would long since have become extinct; there would
be no blessing of family life with its joy of be-
getting, its ever new wonder of birth, its happy
laughter of little children, its unfolding growth into
youth and manhood. In all likelihood there would
have been little human advance, for it is the challenge of love and the family, plus the desire to build
better for our children than you have built for yourselves, that has made for human progress. No
matter how vigorous people might have stayed in
body and even in mind, there would be one vast

unsolvable fact of age on age, complete and irrevocable in its ever hardening antiquity. God knew
what He was doing when He made life; He knew
what He was doing when He planned for physical
death to come at the end of earthly life.

V. FACING DEATH

Then, how should you face death? Face it triumphantly, recognizing the naturalness of physical
death, knowing that in God's providence it is good,
not evil. "If the earthly tent we live in is destroyed,
we have a building from God, a house not made with
hands, eternal in the heavens." Even in the death
of a loved one, you must remember that there are
wonders in store for the godly. Their passing will
be harder to bear than our own but it is written,
"what no eye has seen, nor ear heard, nor the heart
of man conceived, what God has prepared for those
who love him" (1 Cor. 2:9).

The separation from those dear to you will be a
large part of the anguish. Separation is often
necessary if your loved ones are to have a fuller
life, so you send your children off to college or you
give your daughter in marriage and she moves to a
distant city.

Know that Spirit will triumph. This is what St.
Paul meant when he said, "The last enemy to be
destroyed is death." Here our Christian faith
steps in. For the man of God the death and resur-

rection of our Lord Jesus Christ, is the final proof,
'Because I live, you shall live also.''

Death, be not proud, though some have called thee
Mighty and dreadful, for thou art not so:
For those whom thou think'st thou dost overthrow
Die not, poor Death; nor yet canst thou kill me. . .
    One short sleep past, we wake eternally,
    And Death shall be no more: Death, thou shalt die!
                                    —John Donne

Browning, with a vibrant Christian assurance,
could look forward to death as reunion with his
beloved:

        O thou soul of my soul!
        I shall clasp thee again,
        And with God be the rest!

We shall meet one another again; we shall know
one another again. This is the Christian faith.
Finally, you must live by the victorious life of the
Son of God, Who loved us and gave himself for us.

After a long life of outgoing goodness and service,
death came to John Wesley in a quaint little chapel
on City Road, London. In the evening, as friends
stood around his bed, he said to them: ''The best
of all, God is with us.'' On through the night he
kept repeating that; and even after they could no
longer hear him speak, they could still see his lips
forming the words: ''The best of all, God is with
us.''

Your Place in Society . . .

CHAPTER TEN

Jesus, You and the State

From our childhood we have been taught, and rightly, that America was founded by those who were searching for God rather than gold. Truest Christian patriotism has always involved blessings for all mankind, "In thee shall all families of the earth be blessed" (KJV).

> All praise to thee, our Country,
>   Begotten by our sires,
> Where men may worship as they will
>   By freedom's altar fires. . .
> To thee, beloved Country,
>   We give our hearts and hands
> To grant the boon of liberty
>   To all earth's darkened lands.
> In every realm may right prevail,
>   May strife and conflict cease.
> Our Country, lead the waiting world
>   To brotherhood and peace.[1]

States have their place. When rightly understood the state is a means to an end, making possible a system for the enrichment of each citizen. Yet there is a peculiarly damning modern heresy which holds that states are an end in themselves. Much

---

[1] Thomas Curtis Clark.

104

of the agony of the twentieth century has been due to this false philosophy. The world-famous historian, Kenneth Latourette, in speaking of this new concept of the state, says, "For many nationalism became a new religion, a substitute for an abandoned Christianity."[2] We need all the light possible on what should be our attitude to the state.

I. LOVE OF THE STATE

Our Lord was a citizen of the universe, but he was an intense Jew. Most of his fellow-countrymen had a far stronger sense of what we would call national consciousness than many of their contemporaries. It was an outgrowth of their sense of being in a special way "the chosen of God." The modern Jewish scholar, Dr. Julius Morganstern, has said that first-century Judaism was strongly nationalistic. The Gospels record definite racial and national consciousness on the part of Jesus, so much so that at one place he said, "Salvation is of the Jews." He felt a solidarity with his own people.

We hear the words of the Master saying, "O Jerusalem, Jerusalem . . . How often would I have gathered your children together as a hen gathers her brood under her wings, and you would not!" To our Lord, Jerusalem was not only a national capital, but the religious center of his people as well. These words are evidence of the same deep love for his country and its capital city that Jeremiah knew.

---

[2]*The Great Century*, Harper & Brothers, Inc., p. 163.

Aware as Jesus was of solidarity with his own people there is much evidence of universalism on his part. Christian teaching is that Jesus died for all mankind, not for Jews alone.

There is an instinctive love that you have for the place of your birth, for God's good earth whose bountiful bosom has nourished you with its fruitful harvest,

> Breathes there a man
> With soul so dead
> Who never to himself hath said,
> This is my own, my native land.

Your patriotism can and should be both genuine and abiding. Patriotism becomes a vice when your own state is exalted at the expense of a neighboring state. I happen to have been born in Texas. There is a genuine loyalty which every Texan knows to the place of his birth, but this should not lessen in the slightest my love for Indiana, Michigan, and Massachusetts where I have spent the major part of my active ministry. True love and well-being is inclusive rather than exclusive. When a new baby comes into the family, it does not mean that the other children are less loved. The capacity of your heart is enlarged to take in the new arrival. Jesus has given us the inclusive view.

II. PLACE OF THE STATE

On one occasion a group of political leaders tried to snare Jesus on the question of loyalty to his own

people. They asked him the catch question, "Is
it lawful to pay taxes to Caesar or not? Should we
pay them, or should we not?" (Mark 12:14.) Taxes
have never been popular but they were even less
popular then than today, for the fewest benefits
were given in exchange for taxation: no schools, no
parks, no fire protection, and the minimum of roads.
The money went to make fat the collectors, to build
imposing palaces, and to support foreign armies.
The record tells us that Jesus immediately recognized their hypocrisy but at the same time acknowledged that the state has its place. So he asked for
a coin and inquired, "Whose likeness and inscription is this?" They said to him, "Caesar's." Jesus
replied, "Render to Caesar the things that are
Caesar's, and to God the things that are God's"
(Mark 12:16-17). Involved in this exchange of
questions and answers is the fact that Jesus was
anything but an anarchist or nihilist. He knew
that states make possible a society. Therefore
they have their dues. Caesar should have his tax
and should have the loyalty of the people at least
up to a point. Our Lord was as aware as Paul that
a state was better than no state. The acceptance
of coinage is a recognition of sovereignty.

In another place Jesus certainly implied that
courts have their place (Matt. 5:25-26), yet there is
every evidence that he had the common man's attitude toward the law and the whole judicial process.
His advice was to avoid a court trial if at all pos-

sible. His admonition to work for a settlement rather than to face a long lawsuit still has relevance for our day. On still another occasion Jesus made provision to pay his Temple tax (Matt. 17:24f), thereby recognizing fully his duties and obligations to the state. The wisest of his followers have always known that they must take their place in the machinery of the state.

III. OTHER STATES AND PEOPLES

Luke in his seventh chapter records a moving conversation with a Roman centurion of whom our Lord testified, "I tell you, not even in Israel have I found such faith." There is no record of Jesus showing any anti-Roman prejudice or feeling.[3] Concerning his whole relation with foreigners, C. J. Cadoux remarks, "His own personal example and his ethical teaching clearly reveal the solution he advocated. It was that by gentleness, good will, and religious leadership, Israel should change the suspicious tyranny of Rome and the contempt of the Gentile world into a peaceful fellowship, and should thus become the 'guide, philosopher, and friend' of mankind and the builder of a real and world-wide kingdom of God.'"[4]

Observe the relations of Jesus with the Samaritans whose proximity as a neighbor and whose theolog-

---

[3] See: H. Branscomb in *New Testament Studies*. E. P. Booth, p. 220.

[4] *The Expository Times*, Edinburgh, December, 1926, p. 139.

ical deviation were just sufficient to thoroughly an-
tagonize the average Jew. In the fourth chapter of
John where our Lord talks with a woman of
Samaria, Jesus evidences a clear recognition of
Israel's place in God's program. Yet as the dialogue
unfolds, the woman was certainly admitted into
the messianic fellowship. Then there is the marvelous story of the Good Samaritan in which Jesus
went out of his way to select as the hero a Samaritan
who becomes in the story such an illustration of
neighborliness as the world can never forget.

In Mark's seventh chapter where Jesus talks with
the Syrophoenician woman, we have again a clear
recognition of Israel's mission to the world which
our Lord evidenced. Loss of a sense of mission can
be fatal. There is no gain in becoming a so-called
citizen of the world at the expense of local loyalty.

IV. THE KINGDOM OF GOD

Jesus loved his own state. The record that we
have shows him to be a good citizen, supporting its
institutions while recognizing that other peoples
have their place. Yet there was never any doubt
that though Caesar should be rendered Caesar's
coin, nevertheless *God's Kingdom comes first.* One
tragedy of so much modern thought is that men fail
to give God his due in time, effort, and money. Although the United States has been rightly insistent
on the separation between church and state, nearly
all Americans have a sense of fitness when the

church banner is flown above the Stars and Stripes
during divine services aboard naval vessels. It is
a small way of recognizing that allegiance to God
does take precedence over allegiance to the state, a
truth sorely needed in this day of monolithic and
apparently all-demanding states. It is fitting that
the national flag be displayed in our churches, not
to show ties between church and state, but to show
that the state owes its well-being to God, is under
the judgment of God and that the state in penitence
and humility must look to God for guidance. The
average Christian does not agree with the pacifist
or conscientious objector, but he is ready to battle
for their right to their views; for in the final analysis we must always obey the voice of God speaking
to the individual heart rather than that of men.
Those of us who have been raised in the democratic
heritage rightly cherish it, for apparently only in
this system do we have a chance to see that our laws
are in keeping with God's laws.

Jesus proclaimed that the Kingdom is open to
all who have faith, "I tell you, many will come from
east and west and sit at table with Abraham, Isaac,
and Jacob in the kingdom of heaven" (Matt. 8:11).
There is an ultimate universalism about Jesus: all
redeemed men are children of God and therefore
brothers. The author of Revelation caught this
note, "The kingdom of the world has become the
kingdom of our Lord and of his Christ." You can
and should continue your national allegiance, but

you have a larger allegiance to God and His kingdom. Allegiance is inclusive, not exclusive. No better illustration of the inclusiveness that comes to those who rightly understand the teaching of Jesus is seen than in the life and death of John A. Graham, who was born in Scotland and died in Kalimpong in the Himalayas. Dr. Graham founded the homes for Anglo-Indian children at Kalimpong. No European Christian has ever been given a funeral in India such as that accorded Dr. Graham. He was in the small company of choice modern souls who are in the best sense of the term citizens of the world. William Axling, E. Stanley Jones, John R. Mott are world citizens of the kingdom of our Lord and of his Christ. They are devoted followers of Jesus who was loyal to his land and people, but whose first allegiance was ever to God, his Father, whose sun shines and whose rain falls on all men in all nations, the unjust as well as the just.

Your Place in Society . . .

CHAPTER ELEVEN

Jesus, You and Your Work

"A certain man went to his pastor and said he was converted, and asked what he ought to do next. The pastor inquired what the man's occupation was, and learned that he was an engineer. 'Good,' he said; 'the next thing is for you to convert your fireman.' Was he right? . . . It has been said, 'the use of one's occupation as a means for evangelization may very easily involve betraying the call of God, which is to serve Him in our work.' "[1] One of the live questions facing the modern Christian is the matter of vocation. If you are a young person the choice is as vital as your whole future. If you are older you often need to develop right and Christian attitudes about your job.

I. THE CHURCH AND VOCATION

Contrary to popular view, the curse in the Garden of Eden story does not involve the matter of work; rather the otherwise, for Genesis 2:15 tells us that the Lord God put man "in the Garden of Eden to till it and keep it." Work became a curse only when

[1]Ecumenical Studies, *The Laity*, World Council of Churches, Leaflet No. 6.

112

man disobeyed God (Genesis 3:19) and grinding
toil became necessary for mere subsistence.

The ancient Hebrew considered manual work of
such value that every child was taught a trade.
Paul was a tentmaker, Jesus a carpenter. The
wisest men have always known that work, instead
of being a curse, has been a blessing. In our own
country the small town and farm gave a resource-
fulness that we must somehow preserve in American
life. Catherine Bowen in her *John Adams and the
American Revolution* brings out how Adams' toil
on the farm in Quincy helped to give him those ster-
ling qualities of character that were a blessing to
Boston and our nation.

Through the centuries the church has had something positive to say about work or vocation. The
early church questioned the occupation of the
soldier. To the medieval church, banking and the
profession of the actor were looked down upon.
Today it is obvious that dope peddling and prosti-
tution are wrong. The church in all her branches
has seldom hesitated to speak out concerning such
evils. Yet the problem is not always easy. What
should be the attitude of Christians, for instance,
employed by distilleries in Frankfort, Ky.? Their
very livelihood is involved. How can you reconcile
their employment with their religious profession?
Especially is this so with those who are members
of evangelical churches that have taken a definite
stand against the liquor traffic. It was John Calvin

who said: "God has appointed to all their particular duties in different spheres of life . . . Every
individual's line of life, therefore, is, as it were, a
post assigned him by the Lord, that he may not
wander about in uncertainty all his days."[2] There
is no conceivable way you can fit the liquor traffic
into such a judgment.

The modern Christian attitude has been summed
up by the World Council pamphlet referred to
above. "Christians would doubtless all agree that
work must provide a sphere for the service of one's
fellow-men. . . . Must we demand that all man's work
should be such as can be offered to God as the
sacrifice of our hands? What is the proper relation
of work to leisure? Is free time merely a period of
recuperation after work, in order to strengthen us
for more work; or, on the contrary, is work the
means of honorably acquiring enough money to
enable us to make the right use of leisure time?"

II. JESUS A MAN OF TOIL

In going back to the gospel story we find that our
Lord was a man of toil. Joseph was a carpenter
and Jesus worked at this trade (Mark 6:3). The
fact that he worked with his hands endears him to
us. He made furniture, doors, and many of the farm
implements used by the peasants of his time. Most
of his illustrations were taken from the workaday

---

[2]*Interseminary Series,* Book 3, Harper & Bros., Inc., p. 190.

world around him: the sower, the reaper, the vine-dresser, the fisher, the shepherd, and the housewife.

> The yokes He made were true.
> Because the man who dreamed
> Was too
> An artisan,
> The burdens that the oxen drew
> Were light.
> At night
> He lay upon his bed and knew
> No beast of his stood chafing in a stall
> Made restless by a needless gall.[3]

III. LESSONS OUR LORD DREW FROM THE FIELD OF WORK

Jesus was not a labor leader or professor of economics. His teachings about work are all incidental, but they do give an over-all picture that you must take into account. In the parables very few make no reference to work or toil. First we see that *the world's work needs to be done*. The Parable of the Sower involves the universal task of planting which goes on constantly in an agricultural and settled community. In our generation we have sometimes forgotten that our whole industrial economy is ultimately dependent on God's good earth and the bounty it produces after man has toiled laboriously to make the earth bring forth. We plant seeds today by machine rather than cast-

---

[3]Gladys Latchaw, quoted in *Masterpieces of Religious Verse*, Harper & Bros., Inc., No. 535.

ing them abroad as did the Sower, but the seed still
has to be planted and God still makes his rain to fall
and his sun to shine so that there might be a time of
harvest. The parable involves the fact that the
Sower not only works, but there is an Evil one who
also makes the most of his time in sowing weeds.
Again, in the parable of the draw-net there is the
picture of fishermen hard at work bringing in the
wet and silvery horde of fat fish for hungry mankind.

In the Parable of the Talents or Pounds the point
is made that money or *wealth ought to be put to
work*. You must invest your life. Jesus does not
raise the question of the ethical implications of
usury or interest here; he simply tells the story as
it would normally unfold, with the man of property
expecting that his wealth would be gainfully employed during his absence.

In the third place, *work must serve a constructive
purpose*. We see this in the Parable of the Two
Sons. The father's field needed to be tended. One
son shirked his duty, while the other did the necessary tasks. The Christian position has always been
that honest work brings a blessing to mankind. It
was Jeremy Taylor, the seventeenth-century divine,
who said: "His calling itself and the very worldly
employment in honest trades and offices is a serving
of God. . . ." The Master himself did not hesitate to
work on the sabbath when his healing power was so
desperately needed. He quoted scripture to justify

his position, using it in a typical rabbinic fashion: "My Father is working still, and I am working" (John 5:17), a reference to the fact that mankind is still in the epoch of the seventh creative day. When the disciples of Jesus were hungry he allowed them to pluck the grain in a field as they walked. The legalism of his time did not count this a breaking of the regulations, but when the disciples rubbed out the grain in their hands to remove the chaff so that it might be more tasty they were threshing and thus infringing upon the hard legalism of their age! This not only seems foolish to us but it did to Jesus, also. When men had need they should not wait. When you are hungry your food should be as palatable as possible, on the sabbath or on any other day. The sanest of Christians down the centuries have followed our Lord in this wisdom: ". . . It is better to plow upon holy days than to do nothing or to do viciously. . . ."[4]

Jesus was certainly clear in his teaching that *workers should receive adequate pay.* "The laborer deserves his wages" (Luke 10:7). In the Parable of the Vineyard Workers the main lesson is that the kingdom is open to all whether they come early or late. But here is one parable where we might say that there is a strong secondary lesson which involves the fact that those who worked only one hour had as great need for a day's wage as those who had worked all day. This parable must trouble a

---

[4]Jeremy Taylor, in *World's Devotional Classics,* Funk & Wagnalls, p. 7.

certain type of economic royalist. Modern econo-
mists know that American industrial strength has
been built on the purchasing power of the masses.
Paul Reynaud recently pointed this out when com-
paring French production with American. An electric refrigerator of American design made in France
costs 50 per cent more than the same machine made
in our country. Yet wages there are only a third
of what we pay! Give men a sense of belonging to
an economy and they will work far more effectively.

Another teaching of Jesus is that there *should be
joy in the task accomplished*. We see this in the
parables of the Lost Sheep and the Lost Coin.
"Rejoice with me, for I have found my sheep which
was lost"—although it had taken a long, hard night
of tramping to find it. One of our main modern
tasks is to put the joy of creative accomplishment
back into our industrial society. J. H. Oldham
writes: "Men cannot rest satisfied unless they can
find a meaning, or at least some gleam of meaning,
in their work. . . . They should be convinced that
what they are doing, however laborious and exact-
ing, is contributing to the good of the community as
a whole."[5] There must be a larger outlook than
that of the Italian day laborer who was asked why
he dug ditches. "I diga da ditch to buya da bread,
to geta da strength to diga da ditch." Brother
Lawrence found that he could praise God scrubbing

[5] *The Christian and His Occupation*, Federal Council of Churches,
pp. 4, 5.

pots and pans in the kitchen. As far as this writer is concerned, I find I can praise Him better with an electric dishwasher!

Is there any way that you can put meaning into monotonous mass production work? Certainly this is not easy. It may involve more of a philosophical attitude than many workers have, but at least there is value in pointing out an approach. Suppose you are a worker on the assembly line at the Ford Motor Company. There are at least these factors involved:

1. This car which people need and want is absolutely dependent on your tightening these nuts or putting on that steering wheel effectively.
2. You become a vital part of a social and economic whole. The entire process is impossible unless you work effectively with your fellow workers.
3. You get your creative satisfaction out of the *completion of the whole* which you could never do individually, but working with others you can bring it to pass.

Your other creative satisfactions can be provided by home gardening, craftsmanship, music, painting, or possibly work in the church or for the community. You have all heard the old story about the three stone masons at work on a cathedral: When asked what they were doing one replied, "I am working for $2.50 an hour." Another said, "I am putting this stone in place." The third and last got the true meaning of Christian vocation by his reply: "I am building the house of God."

Work is not an end in itself. This is surely involved in the Parable of the Rich Fool. His hard work probably killed him on the night when his soul was required of him. His only solution for his wealth was storage. Bigger barns for bumper crops! How shortsighted, when there was a hungry world around him! He was the biggest fool imaginable for he had fat barns and no one to whom he wished to leave them. No friends on earth, and no treasure in heaven! Some American businessmen and even some church leaders have yet to learn the lesson that work is not an end in itself.

IV. THE MODERN CHRISTIAN MESSAGE ON VOCATION

It is clear from the teachings of our Lord that the Christian has a task: "Come to me, all who labor and are heavy-laden. . . ." There is a heresy evident in some Christian hymns that makes it seem that God calls his followers to a do-nothing existence. Isaac Watts knew this when he wrote:

> Must I be carried to the skies
> on flowery beds of ease,
> While others fought to win the prize
> and sailed through bloody seas?

Some modern hymn writers give the impression that the ultimate ideal for the Christian is lethargic ease. Nothing could be further from the truth. A truer understanding has been that even "in the land that is fairer than day" there are tasks to accomplish for God. Whatever the future may bring, it is certainly true that here Jesus taught, and the keenest of his modern followers know, that work is a blessing that is shared by both God and man. "Man's call from God is to see what God is doing and to share in the labor."[6] "To do needful work, then, to lose oneself and find oneself therein, to participate thus in a common task and a shared life: this and the summons to it, we shall mean by vocation."[7] The message of the church of our Lord Jesus Christ about work is summed up:

1. All work should be honest and industrious.
2. In employment you must have ethical attitude and fair play.
3. Christian faith gives work a meaning: "Christianity demands a society wherein the universal obligation to work is recognized, and all engage in some socially necessary service. It sees work in terms of its spiritual significance as making fulness of life possible for all men."[8]

"The Glory of God may and must be promoted in the family, the daily task and the everyday life. Every aspect of the world's work is thus given a somewhat sacramental status."[9]

[6]D. D. Williams, *God's Grace and Man's Hope*, Harper & Brothers, Inc., p. 145.

[7]Robert Calhoun, *God and Common Life*, Charles Scribner's Sons, p. 71.

[8]*The Laity*, op. cit.

[9]E. G. Homrighausen: *Interseminary Series*, Book 3, Harper & Brothers, Inc., p. 189.

> This is the gospel of labor, ring it, ye bells of the
>   kirk,—
> The Lord of Love came down from above to live with
>   the men who work,[10]

The church must always bear witness to the Christian concern for the common good. This brings us back to the answer of the question we raised at the beginning of the chapter about the first thing that the engineer should do after he became a Christian. In the light of the teaching of our Lord you have the answer: Be the best engineer possible, because people, all of God's people, need regular, efficient transport. Evangelize on the side.

Finally, we ought to work well because Jesus did well his physical tasks, and because Jesus did well the task his Father sent him to do.

> Never in a costly palace did I rest on golden bed,
> Never in a hermit's cavern have I eaten idle bread.
> Born within a lowly stable, where the cattle round
>   me stood,
> Trained a carpenter in Nazareth, I have toiled and
>   found it good.[11]

---

[10]Henry Van Dyke, *Poems of Inspiration*, N. Y., Halcyon House, Copyright, Charles Scribner's Sons.

[11]Henry Van Dyke, *op. cit.*

CHAPTER TWELVE

Jesus, You, and Your Wealth

Do you remember when you were a child clutching two pennies in a hot hand and wistfully looking through the candy counter trying to decide whether to buy one licorice stick or six jelly beans? From that day on, wealth and its use was a problem for you as for all of us. The attitude of Jesus toward wealth is one that should give help. His basic economic principles are as applicable to our day as to his.

I. JESUS' EVALUATION OF MONEY

A Gospel passage tells us that our Lord had not where to lay his head; yet, as a famous itinerant rabbi, he did not worry about housing or food. Jesus and his disciples were welcomed in most villages. Food and lodging were happily shared. Later when his company of disciples grew larger the record mentions that there were women who "ministered" to him (Mark 15:41). They were evidently a group of women of some affluence.

There is indication that Jesus was a systematic manager. For one thing, as the head of his own household, he did not leave home until his mother and younger brothers and sisters could get along by themselves. Evidently things had been managed so carefully that the carpenter shop and small business connected with it could be carried on effectively in his absence.[1] The mention of the common purse that Judas as the treasurer carried is another indication that some degree of care was shown in financial transactions. That Judas later proved to be a thief is beside the point.

From the beginning of society, money of some description has been used as a medium of exchange. This is a fundamental and a legitimate use of money. At a Samaritan village the disciples of Jesus bought food. Our Lord paid his Temple tax. When his enemies put him on the spot by asking if the Roman taxes should be paid, Jesus called for a coin and remarked that Caesar's coins should be given to Caesar at the proper time. But he reminded them that God also has His obligations. There was nothing unusual about the attitude of Jesus toward wealth. He did not hesitate to promise his disciples certain material rewards. "And every one who has left houses or brothers or sisters or father or mother or children or lands, for my name's sake, will receive a hundredfold, and inherit eternal life" (Matt. 19:29). Mark interestingly enough adds "with persecutions" (Mark 10:30). The latter is certainly an authentic note.

---

[1]This, of course, is conjecture, but legitimate conjecture.

In the Parable of the Talents (Matt. 25:14-30) Jesus drives home the truth that goods or wealth must be put to use. Buried money or buried treasure in any form is harmful. This is the reason the rich fool who wanted to build barns was condemned. As a good Jew, Jesus would in all probability have disapproved of interest on money. The rates in those days were exorbitant, often amounting to from 40 per cent to 100 per cent. Jesus' use of this parable is in the same category as that of the Unjust Judge. His reference to interest does not necessarily mean that he approved of the process. The main lesson of the parable is that wealth put to use is blessed by God; that the owner of the money profited to a degree of which he would disapprove is simply an incident of the story. It has no bearing on our Lord's feeling about usury. In other places Jesus tells in no uncertain terms what he thinks of the rich.

Jesus had the peasant's understanding of the true value of money. We see this in the story of the woman who lost a coin and swept the house until she found it (Luke 15). The coin as a part of the bridal dowry had far greater value to the woman than its intrinsic worth. On another occasion Jesus watched worshipers as they cast gifts into the Temple treasury. When he saw the widow slip in her two mites he remarked that her gift weighed more than the gifts of many who had cast in fortunes. The measure of helpfulness for God's cause is determined by largeness of heart.

II. JESUS CASTIGATES THE ABUSE OF MONEY

We immediately think of the Parable of the Rich Fool as we see how Jesus spoke out vigorously against *private abuse of goods* (Luke 12:16-21). Here was wealth used in a completely selfish project—"Soul . . . take your ease." Walter Horton's historical analysis underscores what Jesus taught so plainly, "The passion for amassing wealth is a symptom that civilization is beginning to decline again into barbarism."[2] As we have observed, the tragedy of the rich fool is seen in its ultimate *denouement* (Luke 12:20), where he had no friends on earth and no treasure in heaven!

In the incident of the cleansing of the Temple, Jesus spoke and acted against the *public abuse of money* as he upset the tables of the money-changers (Matt. 21:12-13). Here were a group of men fattening on a politically provided monopoly. In passing we can remark that state socialism or government ownership is not necessarily the answer to the problems created by wealth. Not until you have truly redeemed men running a state or a business will you solve the problem. These particular men were rendering a public service, but at a profiteering gain to themselves. Spiritual worship was almost

---

[2]*Can Christianity Save Civilization?* Harper & Bros., Inc., p. 20.

impossible after dealing with them. Jesus rightly turned the rascals out.

In connection with the Prodigal Son, Jesus gave by implication a warning about the *personal abuse of money*. It was wealth that helped to ruin the boy. Not until his money was gone was there hope of salvation. This personal problem was solved by his return to his father, or, in other words, by redemption.

III. JESUS AND THE RICH

In the story of the beggar Lazarus asking a crust at the gate of the rich man (Luke 16:20-31) is a dramatic incident with the rich and the poor used as a foil. On the surface the story apparently condemns one man because of his wealth and praises the other because of his poverty. This view is one that was customary in the prophetic tradition, and certainly one to which Jesus would not be unsympathetic. But the real meaning of the parable is that human evaluation of wealth and poverty is completely reversed in spiritual reality.

In the account of the Rich Young Ruler, his wealth was a definite barrier to spiritual advancement. Jesus himself generalized the incident by saying that it is easier for a camel to go through the eye of a needle than for a rich man to enter the Kingdom of Heaven. Here our Lord was postulating an impossibility. All homiletical attempts to suggest a small gate called a "needle's eye" through which

a camel could squeeze break down on the hard
archeological facts that there were *no such small
gates* in the time of Jesus. Jesus concludes the
story that with God all things are possible by showing how even the wealthy had a chance. Yet John
Macmurray rightly observes, "There is no way of
escape from recognizing not merely that Jesus
believed in the common people, but that he also dis-
believed in the wealthy, and that he saw in their
wealth the real barrier between them and the community of mankind which it was his mission to
establish."[3] What Jesus is saying is that no man
has enough wealth to get to heaven. John D. Rockefeller, Senior, told an interesting story on himself.
He was a faithful member of the Euclid Avenue
Baptist Church of Cleveland. One day in driving
home after church he recognized one of the Sunday
school girls walking home. He told his chauffeur to
stop and pick her up. The big limousine drove up
beside the child and John D. Rockefeller rolled
down the window and said, "Jump in, I'll drive you
home." Not at all certain about the identity of the
important-looking stranger, the child remembered
the warning of her mother never to accept rides
from strange men. Yet she did not want to hurt
the feelings of the one who was kind enough to offer
her a lift so with a child's naïveté she replied to
the head of the Standard Oil Company of America,
"No, thank you, I'm afraid you do not have enough

[3]*Creative Society*, Association Press, p. 71.

gasoline to take me home"! Jesus knew that we get into the Kingdom of Heaven by the grace of God, not by the size of our bankbooks or the amount of oil we possess.

The Master's wise understanding of money and its true relation to life is seen in the story of Zacchaeus. In contrast to the rich young ruler, Jesus did not disturb his physical possessions because he had his heart.

IV. JESUS AND THE POOR

Our Lord delighted in his ministry to the *am-ha-aretz*—"men of the land." He said, "The poor have good news preached to them." The rich and powerful could always have a sponsor. Jesus was on the side of the common people as the greatest religious leaders have always been: Moses, Amos, St. Francis of Assisi, the young Luther, John Wesley, and Walter Rauschenbusch. It was Jesus who really discovered the common man. It was his great contribution to social history, for the rights of the little man are the foundation stones of democracy.

V. JESUS AND GIVING

Jesus commended a widow for giving her mite. He knew what it meant for the poor to give, for he was poor himself. But he also knew the privilege of having a part in the support of God's Kingdom. Our Lord would not deny the widow that joy, and

the implication, of course, is that you ought to give
until it hurts. Jesus, as a good Jew, knew what i
meant to tithe. On one occasion he criticized cer
tain men who tithed "mint and dill and cummin.'
But he went on, "These you ought to have done
without neglecting the others." Our Lord taugh
that each of us has a personal responsibility in ou
giving. There is an unusual blessing in wealth tha
is shared. We close with one of the floating say
ings of Jesus which did not find its way into th
Gospels but happily is preserved for us in the Boo
of Acts. St. Paul is urging the Ephesian church t
generosity when he admonishes them to remembe
"the words of the Lord Jesus, how he said, 'It i
more blessed to give than to receive' " (Acts 20:35)

Your Place in the Church . . .

CHAPTER THIRTEEN

Your Church and the Creativeness Jesus Gives

A study of the solution that Jesus brings to the problems of life could stop with the previous chapter, but that would leave you in many respects in the first century, or in any century. Is there guidance from the Way that transforms every generation which has special relevance to the specific time in which you and I live? This chapter and the next speak to that issue. In this chapter the corporate answer is given as we outline hope for the church in which the individual merges his personality "in Christ" with all who love our Lord.[1]

The great depression left many vivid memories and experiences. One of the most revealing incidents that I recall is connected with the story of Mario Izzo, an Italian immigrant who, like millions of others, was on relief. There was something in his very nature which made it impossible for him to accept money without giving value returned. On his own initiative, he purchased a broom and began

[1]This chapter is adapted from an address delivered at the One Hundredth Anniversary of the International Convention of Disciples of Christ, meeting in Cincinnati, Ohio, in October, 1949.

to sweep the streets of Aliquippa, Pennsylvania, where he lived. When interviewed by reporters, who learned of his action in voluntarily assuming a task to which he was not obligated, he said, "I looka da check and think this is a wonderful country. I decida be honest man with this country which has been so good to me, so I starta sweep da street. My bread it taste sweet, and I feela lika a man, because I work." Here is a dramatic incident in our time of the same type of creative response to a difficult situation that has made America great. Arnold Toynbee, in his monumental *Study of History*, says, "Civilizations, it would seem, grow through an élan which carries them from challenge through response to further challenge."[2] This same growth as a result of creative response to a challenging situation is as true in the field of religion as in that of civilization.

I. CREATIVENESS IN PROPHETIC RELIGION

Creativeness in religion is seen to a remarkable degree in connection with the history of the Hebrews. They believed that Jehovah had chosen their forefathers, who were led by Moses, and traveled with them to Canaan. A god who was a god of a certain people in a certain locality was no new thing in that day. Creativeness in religion entered when

---

[2] Arnold Toynbee, *The Study of History*, Oxford University Press, p. 189.

the Israelites felt that though Jehovah was traveling with them to Canaan, he remained, strangely also, the God of Sinai. So Elijah goes back to the "Mount of God" for spiritual strength. Creativeness entered the picture as the Israelites saw that the One who could be God of both Sinai and Canaan, could also be God of all of the universe, and so monotheism was established. Creativeness continued in the great eighth-century prophets as Amos and Hosea taught that this same Jehovah was both moral and forgiving to the utmost.

The Israelites were transformed by this concept. They became God's chosen people. "You are . . . my servant whom I have chosen" (Isa. 43:10). In the development of their religious and national consciousness, this possessiveness by God gave them a feeling of exclusiveness, which became their nemesis. In the city of Detroit, when the suburb of Highland Park erected boundary signs saying, "You are now entering the city of lower taxes," the Detroit City Council voted to put up counter-signs: "You are now leaving Detroit, where life is worth living." Some such rejoinder always happens if you advertise exclusiveness!

The creative genius of the Hebrew people reached its zenith with the coming of Christ. "But when the time had fully come, God sent forth his Son," but the people were more enamored of exclusiveness than they were of creativeness.

II. THE CREATIVENESS OF JESUS

Jesus took the concept of Messiah—one whose fan is in his hand—and transformed it into One who would suffer and redeem. He found the concept of "Son of man" as a hazy deliverer who would come on the clouds and out of the sea, and elevated it, "For the Son of man came to seek and to save the lost." Claude Montefiore, the great Jewish scholar, said of Jesus' creativeness, "But to seek out the sinner, and, instead of avoiding the bad companion, to choose him as your friend, in order to work his moral redemption, this was, I fancy, something new in the religious history of Israel . . . it inaugurated a new idea: the idea of redemption, the idea of giving a fresh object of love and interest to the sinner, and so freeing him from sin. The rescue and deliverance of the sinner through pity and love and personal service—the work and the method seem alike due to the teacher of Nazareth."[3]

What was the response of the religious leaders to this new creative concept? It was rejection. Jesus underscored this in his poignant Parable of the Lord's Vineyard, in which he showed how the nation and the people had failed. The servants of Jehovah were repulsed. The prophets were stoned and, as a final indignity, the Son, Himself, was killed.

---

[3]*Some Elements of the Religious Teaching of Jesus*, London, Macmillan, 1910, pp. 57-58.

What had happened? Creativeness was rejected. This was no new thing. It has been a pattern down the centuries, as Professor Toynbee shows: "The gift of creativity becomes in its turn a new and uniquely formidable challenge" to further progress.[4] The minority that has brought advance feels it has vested interests and rests on its laurels. This fact has been underscored in our time by the demise of *The Literary Digest*. So Judaism rejected the creativeness that was in Jesus. "They drave great nails in hands and feet, And made a Calvary."

III. CREATIVENESS IN THE CHURCH

Not all of the Jews refused to accept the religious genius which they saw in Jesus of Nazareth. Those who formed the Christian Church turned the rejection of Christ into a triumph. The stone which the builders rejected did become the head of the corner. The Christian Church, today, is the one world-wide organization firmly dedicated to the proposition of freedom and justice for all. It is built upon God's righteousness and His concern for all men. Some of our keenest modern poets have seen it, for instance Louis MacNeice:

> And man is a spirit
> And symbols are his meat,
> So pull not down the steeple
> In your monied street.

---

[4]*Op. cit.*, pp. 307f, 317.

> For money chimes feebly,
> Matter dare not sing—
> Man is a spirit
> Let the bells ring.[5]

Today the Church may not be accomplishing what many of her protagonists would wish, but she is making a tremendous impact. "There can be no doubt that within these past thirty years, when it has been threatened by gigantic and hostile forces the Gospel has made itself felt more widely among mankind than ever before,"[6] writes Kenneth Latourette, the world's leading church historian.

The International Missionary Council, in reporting on the last twenty-three years' progress on the missionary fields, has revealed some startling figures of advance. Protestants have grown from 6,500,000 to 25,300,000 in this period. Only eternity can measure what has been accomplished in changing lives. Here is just one example from missionary annals as told by Joseph Robbins when foreign mission secretary for American Baptists: Before the turn of the century, Marcus Mason, with his companion, Mr. Phillips, went into the Garo Hills of North India. After fifty years of service, the Garos presented him with a medal commemorating his ministry among them. On it was this inscription: "When he came, he found us savage head

[5]"Holes in the Sky," N. Y., Random House, Inc.

[6]*Christian Outlook*, Harper & Bros., Inc., p. 80; See also: Inter seminary Series, Vol. 2, p. 84f.

hunters. When he left, he left us children of the living God.''

In the Old Testament there is a very descriptive phrase: ''Jeshurun waxed fat, and kicked.'' Like many civilizations, the Church, as it became surfeited, grew in arrogance, so even the Christian Church that had preserved the best of Hellenistic civilization and given birth to our western culture, became, herself, corrupt and sterile. After centuries Protestantism arose as a new creative wine. It had to be placed in new bottles. This meant that the one universal church was now divided, but only in this way could come health. The creative response of the great reformers was necessary to the well-being of the church universal. Luther, Calvin, and Hubmaier would certainly have been shocked, however, if they could have seen the modern proliferation of denominations. We have multiplied until it has become a scandal of Christendom.

Observe a typical response of two great bodies— the Baptists and the Disciples of Christ. Restoration is a glorious word that Disciples have given Christendom. Their plea for the restoration of the primitive church is a good one when rightly understood and exercised. There is a certain nostalgia for the past we all have, the golden age and ''The old time religion'' that was ''Good for Paul and Silas'' and ''. . . good for my old mother, is good enough for me.''

This plea is a definite evidence of vitality and progress. It was a creative response to the new situation of the frontier. The reaction of pioneer Disciples to the challenge of Alexander Campbell and Barton Stone was magnificent. In Campbell, Disciples probably gave to America her greatest creative religious genius. A capital illustration is Campbell's reaction to the organization of their brotherhood. More than any other man, he furnished the impetus to their independent, congregational and almost atomistically minded churches. Yet, after twenty years of the loosest fellowship, his creative mind saw the necessity for closer cooperation, so in the *Millenial Harbinger* for 1842, he wrote: "We can do comparatively little to elevate the christian ministry (or advance) the great missionary field of the world, either at home or abroad, without cooperation. . . . We can have no thorough cooperation without a more ample, extensive, and thorough church organization."

Observe the Baptist response: Baptists believed that they, too, were restoring the primitive church, but the word "restoration" is not a part of their religious vocabulary. All Christendom knows how Baptists responded creatively to the new challenge of Christian missions. There is a great deal of significance in the fact that the modern missionary movement was begun by Baptists; in America, under the impact of supporting Adoniram Judson, and in England, due to the genius of William Carey.

When a young man Carey spoke strongly for the evangelization of the world before the Northampton "Ministers' Fraternal." Dr. Ryland had baptized Carey and, consequently, felt a spiritual father's personal interest, yet he remained in the iron grip of a rigid hyper-Calvinism. As Carey concluded, Ryland sprang up and cried out vehemently, "Young man, sit down, sit down! When God pleases to convert the heathen, He'll do it without your help or mine."

True "restoration" is not returning to primitive conditions. That is sentimental, as well as impossible. Rousseau's child of nature, his "noble savage," *is a child*. True "restoration" is returning to the spirit, the élan, that gave transforming power in the first place.

The final goal for Christians is wrapped up in the assurance of God: "Behold, I make all things new." Real greatness is shown by continuing to make a creative response. The history of civilizations shows that if you are creative in one age you are often the stand-pat conservative of the next. Our western culture is at stake unless we can reverse this process and politically be creative *for our day. Tragedy comes when you fail to make the adequate response*. This is the favorite theme of Greek dramatists, the Agamemnon of Aeschylus and the Oedipus of Sophocles. Now creative response must be made by the modern church; and the church can make the response, *if she will,* for ours is pre-eminently the gospel of the second chance. "Repent, and be baptized every one of you in the name of Jesus Christ for the forgiveness of your sins; and you shall receive the gift of the Holy Spirit."

IV. CREATIVENESS FOR OUR DAY

What is creativeness for our day? It is not a monolithic structure of an overarching church that suppresses all difference and all varied guidance of the Holy Spirit. We had that once in Rome, and there was no soundness in it. Christ's church is inclusive, not exclusive. Did not our Lord say, "Do not forbid him . . . he that is not against us is for us"?

Creativeness consists in being the growing edge of humanity. The church must fill this role as well as continue to be a conscience to the world. T. S. Eliot sees this:

Why should men love the Church? Why should they love her laws?
She tells them of Life and Death, and of all they would forget.
She is tender where they would be hard, and hard where they like to be soft.
She tells them of Evil and Sin, and other unpleasant facts.
They constantly try to escape
From the darkness outside and within
By dreaming of systems so perfect that no one will need to be good.[7]

_____

[7]*Collected Poems*, 1909-1935, Part VI, "The Rock," Harcourt Brace & Co., N. Y., pp. 196, 197.

Creativeness consists in the recognition of our own essential oneness in Christ, for if we do not recognize it, the world will never know it. Within this oneness, creativeness preserves the emphases that have given Protestants their strength.

Creativeness for Christians consists in not only recognizing our oneness, but also in demonstrating to the world that we are one people. Let us show that Christ has not prayed in vain, "that they may all be one; even as thou, Father, art in me, and I in thee, that they also may be in us, so that the world may believe that thou hast sent me."

Now situations change, in churches, as well as lives, and you have to present an adequate response for the circumstances in which you find yourself. Did you read of the probationer in Little Rock, Arkansas, who wrote the Federal Parole Board a glowing letter to prove that he was now reformed and a law-abiding citizen, and noted that "I haven't been in any trouble, except now I am married!" Well, the circumstances that called forth Protestant separateness have changed. May we have the wisdom and the grace of God to change, to serve adequately the men of our day and generation.

Is there a blueprint for a united church? you ask. The answer is "Yes," as long as we remember that we are dealing with an organism, a thing that has life and that must grow if it is to reach maturity. We cannot accomplish it overnight. There are stages in growth through which the church must pass. Such growth certainly involves the reunion of family groups, such as the Reformed and churches of the Presbyterian background. There is no fundamental reason why Methodists should not reunite with Episcopalians. Lutheran bodies can certainly merge if they will. Congregational and other free churches have much in common and will be increasingly drawn together. There are no major matters of doctrine or church policy to hinder Baptists and Disciples from uniting; only the will is lacking.

The second phase in the blueprint for a creative response to the churches in the present world situation is a strengthening of the ecumenical movement, particularly as it is made concrete in the World Council of Churches. Here is a new and opening challenge to Christianity which, we are happy to say, Christians are facing constructively. Dr. Latourette writes of it: "The trend toward a supranational Protestantism, indeed toward a supranational Christianity of world dimensions, is so strong that it is overshadowing the dangerous proclivities toward nationalism ... after World War I, the Ecumenical tie had grown. Here, then, a new kind of Christianity is emerging out of historic Protestantism . . . the trend does not mean a departure from the Gospel, but a firm resolution to emphasize it."[8]

---

[8]*Op. cit.*, p. 156.

Is it too much to dream that the third phase emerging from the cooperative response in the ecumenical movement will be the definite organization of a U.C., a *United Churches,* which will be even more inclusive and effective than a Council of Churches? It could well point the way of cooperation to the U.N., the United Nations, and finally bring peace on earth and good will to men. As with the United Nations, some sovereignty must be given up by the united family groups of churches. In the *United Churches,* the Christian ministry must have mutual recognition and standing. Laymen must be trained to realize a sense of oneness in Christ with all of God's people in any church. Ministers ought to be able to transfer, under the calling of God, from place of service to place of service, with an ordination for one that is an ordination for all. As they move to a new community our Christian families ought to have an inner persuasion that the church which they find there is Christ's church, a member of the *United Churches.* Would not an ultimate Christian position be never to raise the question as to that church's background, whether it was originally Presbyterian, Methodist, Disciple, Episcopal or, is it too much to expect, even a Catholic church?

A weary humanity is far in advance of its political leaders in recognizing its oneness with other men in distant parts of the globe. This was underscored for me in Europe in the summer of 1948. We were on our way to Amsterdam, to attend the ses-

sions of the World Council of Churches. Mrs
Straton and I took a side pilgrimage to Mont St.
Michel, the famous medieval abbey built on an is-
land off the coast of France. For a part of the
journey, from Follyn to Pontorson, we rode by
choice in a third-class carriage. Packed on every
side were the common people of France; their dress
was different, their customs different, their language different. Just across from us was a French
sailor, with his wife and their baby of eight months.
It was not long before I had that baby on my lap,
and the baby responded to affection as do all babies
with a big smile. It again emphasized the fact that
babies, whether French, American, or Hottentot,
are the same throughout the whole earth. So are
all the little ones for whom Christ died. We are
one in God's concern and in Christ's redemption.
What we need is grace to recognize it.

Hope for the church and hope for mankind depends on our response to this new challenge. If it
is creative, if it shows willingness to follow the Holy
Spirit into new areas of advance, there is hope; if
not, we will see fulfilled the nemesis of a Bertrand
Russell, with his race on which "a slow, sure doom
falls pitiless and dark."

It is Arnold Toynbee, however, not Russell, who
holds the last word. He points out the miracle of
the conversion of the American Negro to Christianity as a latter-day triumph of missionary activity.
The appeal of Christianity was such that even

though it was the nominal religion of those who enslaved, its basic teaching of freedom for all in Christ Jesus, our Lord, was such that the heart of the Negro even in his dark bondage knew it had the seeds of redemption in it. "As He died to make men holy, let us die to make men free . . . His truth is marching on." This leading historian writes: "The sap of life is visibly flowing once again through all the branches of our Western Christendom . . . we may yet live to see a civilization that has tried and failed to stand alone being saved, in spite of itself, from a fatal fall by being caught up in the arms of an ancestral church. . . . A tottering civilization which has shamefully succumbed to the intoxication of a showy victory over physical nature, and has applied the spoils to laying up treasure for itself without being rich toward God, may be reprieved from the sentence . . . an apostate Western Christendom may be given grace to be born again as a *Republica Christiana* which was its own earlier and better ideal of what it should strive to be. Is such spiritual rebirth possible?"[9] Toynbee's reply is "Yes."

The creative response, however, must be made by you and by me. If we do not make it, it is not going to be made. In Carl Sandburg's *The Prairie Years* is the story of Lincoln and a Chicago lawyer. In the early 1850's, the two lawyers spent the night in the

[9]Arnold Toynbee, *op. cit.*, pp. 407, 547.

same hotel room. For half the night they sat up in their nightshirts, arguing.

"At last we went to sleep," said the lawyer from Chicago, "and early in the morning, I woke up, and there was Lincoln, half sitting up in bed. 'Dicky,' he said, 'I tell you this nation cannot *exist half slave and half free.*' " There we get the challenging phrase which Abraham Lincoln used later in his debates with Stephen Douglas. Somewhat sheepishly, the Chicago lawyer admitted that his reply was, "Oh, Lincoln, go to sleep!"

So often that is the world's solution. It has never been the solution of the creative greathearts of this earth. It is not God's solution, nor should it be ours.

Your Place in the Church . . .

CHAPTER FOURTEEN

Your Church and the World Vision Jesus Gives

You will observe that the present chapter goes from the second to the first person. The author is thoroughly persuaded that Jesus helps mightily in solving your problems. I know this because he has helped me. This chapter originally grew out of a request to join a distinguished company of theologians and religious leaders in a symposium in the *Christian Century* on "How My Mind Has Changed in the Past Decade."[1] I feel sure that I was selected, not through any eminence, but rather the otherwise, because I represented how an average minister can be molded by the Master Potter when there is an honest effort to discover the mind of Christ. Consequently the following is more in the nature of a personal testimony of what Jesus has done for me and therefore what he can do for you.

---

[1] Articles in the series appeared in 1949: March 9, 16, Karl Barth; March 23, Nels Ferré; March 30, Buell Gallagher; April 20, Walter M. Horton; May 18, Fulton Oursler; June 1, George Barrois; June 15, Paul Tillich; July 6, Emil Brunner; July 20, Philip Bernstein; July 27, John Mackay; October 26, Hillyer H. Straton. Used here by permission of the copyright owner, The Christian Century Foundation.

You are a product of your antecedents and your
environment. Your environment is subject to some
degree of personal control, but your antecedents
remain a constant. You cannot escape blood loyal-
ties, nor would you. Yet a choice is not simple;
often it involves "whether to follow the stars by
which your fathers traveled or whether to follow
the route marked by their dead campfires."

A pastor's pilgrimage will be different from that
of a theologian, a Christian educator, or a religious
executive. It will be guided by the needs of his people, his church, his denomination and his inter-
church connections. An evidence of it should be
found most clearly in his preaching.

I. PREACHING PILGRIMAGE

For more than twenty-five years, I have been an
active pastor, have preached regularly every Sunday, and have kept faithfully all of my old sermons.
One can imagine no finer source for deflating spiritual pride than going back over them occasionally!
If a message fifteen years ago seemed so marvelous
and is now so evidently dull, what about the present
masterpieces? But you remember that God is pa-
tient and your people are most understanding and
long-suffering. In looking over the sermons there
is the development in technical ability which you
would expect, but there is also an indication of
growth in other areas as well. One often has to go
back more than ten years to recognize, however, a

definite trend. In 1932, I preached the annual sermon for the Indiana Baptist Convention; its title was, "A Whole Gospel for the Whole World." The text was the Great Commission as found in Matthew and the sermon had a stylized three points: (1) The power of Jesus; (2) The program of Jesus; (3) The presence of Jesus. Really, it was much better than it sounds! The first point contained a rather caustic criticism of general denominational ineffectiveness, plus a plea for theological regularity. The second emphasized the obvious: go, teach, and observe of the text. The third point was a plea for consecration in the presence of Christ. In 1938, I was asked by the leader of the Fundamentalist Fellowship of the Northern Baptist Convention to bring a message before that body entitled, "The Social Implications of Our Evangelism." Somewhat significantly, the deliverance of this address, which was orthodox enough, occasioned the beginning of our mutual withdrawal from one another. Up to that time, this fellowship in Northern (now American) Baptist circles would be characterized as "His Majesty's Loyal Opposition," but it was rapidly becoming so schismatic in character that many who had worked with it felt the necessity to quietly withdraw.

In 1941, I delivered an address before our Northern Baptist Convention entitled, "Are Our Baptist Publications Adequate?" The answer was "yes," primarily because it is the spirit of loyalty to God's Word and God's Son which really matters.

On return from representing Northern Baptists at Amsterdam, the message reporting the first Assembly of the World Council of Churches was entitled "The Coming World Church." It made the following points: There was "no Pentecost" at Amsterdam. The church was not born there. There were no cloven tongues of flame, for we were not interested in the visibility of the Spirit (that had its place in Jerusalem at the first Pentecost), but we were vitally interested in the fruits of the Spirit, "Love, joy, peace, long-suffering. . . ." However, those of us who were there believed that *the church was born again at Amsterdam,* and this is the factor that has relevance for our generation. The message emphasized two facts: First, that we were there at all, 135 different church bodies meeting as one; second, that the ecumenical pronouncements of the Council were most significant: Jesus Christ is alive. Our unity is real. Old orders are under God's judgment. The world must be won for Christ.

In the above review, there is evidence of the following progression: We start with a narrow sectarianism which is even critical of one's own group but exhibits a complete loyalty to God's revealed truth, especially as seen in Jesus Christ. This loyalty to whole truth is shown by the growing recognition of the social message in a full gospel. We go on to the place the denomination occupies in witnessing to this whole truth. We finally arrive at the full ecumenical position in which there is utter devotion to Jesus Christ as the complete embodiment of revelational truth and to the recognition that all who name his name are one in him.

II. PASTORAL PILGRIMAGE

After the seminary my first full pastorate was with the First Baptist Church of Muncie, Indiana—the Middletown of sociological fame. I was called from there to the First Baptist Church of Detroit, the mass-production capital of the world, soon to become the arsenal of democracy. After seven glorious years (at least for me!) I moved to the First Baptist Church of Malden, a suburb of Boston, the hub of the universe. Whether this is advance, one can judge for oneself! You cannot live and work with and for people without having your personality deepened and mellowed. Such has been the case. The passion to preach is none the less, but the concern of the shepherd is even more. As one has matured in the ministry, more time, rather than less, has been spent with people in their joys as well as their sorrows. Starting as an evangelical with very low-church views, in the past decade I have seen both the value of and the need for liturgy, while maintaining, I trust, the warmth of evangelical positions.

III. THEOLOGICAL PILGRIMAGE

There has been no basic change in my revelational concepts. The vertical dimension has remained constant. God has ever been in my thinking the same: Creator, Sustainer, Revealer, and Redeemer. The views which I hold today can be broadly classified as those that are in the great stream of the Christian tradition. As a good Baptist, I continue to be wary of man-made creeds, yet if I were asked for a creedal expression, I would not hesitate to state as my own faith the affirmations given to the world at Nicaea. As at the beginning of my ministry, so now, "I believe in God, the Father Almighty . . . and in Jesus Christ, His Son, born of the Virgin Mary. . . ." Here is one of those cases where one trusts that he is still traveling by the stars that guided his forefathers.

Any change in theology has been in the horizontal plane. It has been recognized that God desires more than assent, "The devils believe and tremble"; God requires more than religious observances, "I hate, I despise your feasts, and I take no delight in your solemn assemblies." The horizons of my faith have enlarged to take in all of the little ones for whom Christ died and to be incensed as was he at any evil—social, economic, or political—that would destroy and warp human personality. My appreciation of the so-called "social gospel" has been based simply on a deepening understanding of biblical teaching.

In 1940, an article appeared in the *Christian Century*, entitled, "Orthodoxy—A New Phase," and in 1944, "Conservatism States Its Case," in *Religion in Life.* In both I developed more at length the general positions which I find I still maintain. They contained a brief survey of conservative views, with a rationale for traditional Christian positions. The new note in these papers was an equal appreciation for liberalism and its contributions to modern Christian thinking. The dangers of both modernism and fundamentalism were pointed out, and a plea was made for essential Christian views. The term, "modern orthodoxy," rather than "neo-orthodoxy," was employed. About this time I began a serious study of the person of Jesus. A deepening knowledge and understanding of the Man of Nazareth as Son-of-Man and consequently as Son-of-God eventuated. This was seen in two articles in *Christendom,* "What Jesus Thought About Himself" and "The Ecumenical Church and the Worship of Jesus." This study I have continued. The deity of Jesus, held as devoutly as ever, is no longer a simple other-worldly concept. It is now rooted firmly in history and tied intimately with his own messianic consciousness as Son-of-Man and Suffering Servant of the Remnant.

In recent years, a detailed, careful and analytical study of the miracles of Jesus has shaken not at all my former belief in miracle concept, but the study[2] has given a far clearer understanding of what it means to have a faith that moves mountains. For one thing, I see that the power of God cannot neatly

[2]These studies appeared in book form under the title: *Preaching the Miracles of Jesus,* Abingdon-Cokesbury, 1950.

be tied in any small bundle of explanation. There is no rationale for miracle. It has its own category, the category of faith. At the basis of essential Christian belief are three elements of ultimate discontinuity. None of them can finally be explained or accounted for, save on the basis of faith. They are: (1) Redemption; (2) The resurrection of Jesus; (3) Immortality.

The first, redemption, does have some elements which the psychologists say are explainable and yet the whole Christian thesis that a Man on a cross provides redemption for all who will believe on Him is in the realm of faith. Though we cannot ultimately account for it, as we look about we see countless evidences of redemption. We know people who are born again. The resurrection of Jesus can no more be accounted for in its final essence than can redemption. All New Testament evidence supports the record of the resurrection of Jesus with such a powerful witness that the most careful and exact scholars admit that there was some extraordinary phenomenon which took place. Psychologically and historically you cannot account for the church apart from the resurrection of Jesus. Though everyday experience tells us that a man could not come back from the dead, theological and Christian experience tells us that the resurrection of Jesus is not contrary to what God can and did do. Immortality is wholly subjective, completely in the realm of faith; Christian assurance steps in here and as with redemption and the resurrection of Jesus says that because he lives, we too shall live. None of these three basic factors of Christian understanding can ultimately be explained. Their category is one of faith. They are believed. It is faith that "God so loved the world that he gave his only Son . . ." for us men and our redemption. This has not changed. If it ever does, it will be a dark day for the world.

IV. BIBLICAL PILGRIMAGE

It is evident from the above that my theological views have been and are largely influenced by biblical concepts. The conservative position, as I received it in my home and in the seminary, was not that of plenary inspiration. The Bible was the Word of God, and it was true, but it should be rightly interpreted in the light of all scripture, which was written by "holy *men* of old," not angels. Common sense in understanding the Bible was a large factor. However, my views toward the Bible were naïve, not a product of systematized thinking. At the same time, the naïve view did tend toward the docetic with an emphasis on the other-worldly, if I may borrow Christological concepts. As I delved more deeply into a study of the Bible, its text and its background, the place that men had in its composition became ever clearer. In using the same Christological analogy, I avoided Pelagianism which makes the Bible solely a product of man's

search and aspirations by recognizing that "holy
men of God *spake as they were moved by the Holy
Spirit.*" This view has paralleled the strong movement in both Europe and the United States that
gives increasing recognition to the Bible as the revelation of God and the source of Christian knowledge. Unquestionably, much of the revival that we
have experienced in Christianity in recent years
has been this rediscovery of the Bible as the eternal
Word of the living God.

In the late 1930's Hendrick Kraemer coined the
phrase, "Biblical realism." It happily describes
the positions advocated by the greatest theological
thinkers of our generation: Karl Barth, Reinhold
Niebuhr, Emil Brunner, Nels Ferré, Walter Horton,
and a host of others. There is not space here to
expand on this view, which has nothing in common
with biblicism on one hand, or humanism on the
other. My thinking has been influenced by this
whole trend, which I believe with all my heart to
be the truth. For me, it has been the triumph of
the Athanasian as regards the Bible as against
docetism and Pelagianism, if one still may be allowed
to continue the analogy. Along with the acceptance of scientific and critical contributions to biblical knowledge has gone an advanced understanding and appreciation of the Bible, which one could
never have had otherwise. It is not a new Book to
me, but it is a far more meaningful Book. It is
more, instead of less, the Word of God than ever

before. With even greater vehemence than in my precritical days, I can join the unlettered man of Faith in saying, "I believe the Bible from Generations to Revolutions!"

Instead of the gates being lowered to unbelief by a recognition of the Divine-human character of the Bible, rather the opposite is the case, for no longer do you have to defend the Word on untenable ground. The acceptance of this position, which I believe to be truest to scripture, has not lessened one iota the vertical dimensions of my faith in God and in His Son, Christ Jesus the Lord. God is still the One who is high and lifted up. As I continue to look upon that strange Man hanging there on a cross because of his devotion to his heavenly Father, I see how expansive was the love of God and how great His concern that men might have life and have it abundantly as He works through the man Christ Jesus His wonders to perform. My theology, my Christology now is higher, not lower, than it was ten years ago.

V. ECUMENICAL PILGRIMAGE

Ten years ago I began work on a manuscript which was published under the title: *Baptists: Their Message and Mission.* Behind this was a heritage of seven generations of Baptist ministers on my mother's side and two on my father's. This popular study of Baptist faith and practice, instead of enhancing a sectarian view, had the opposite effect. The final chapter, entitled, "Where We Are Going?" concluded with a plea for the coming church universal. The Preface, written after the completion of the volume, has the following statement: "Cooperative endeavor can only come as we appreciate the history and the hopes that have characterized our various denominations. We can never learn to work together until we know how we work separately." This deeper understanding of one's own history and background has made for a more expansive, rather than a more narrow, view of the church universal. This seemingly paradoxical fact has been true of the ecumenical movement as a whole.

When I began my pastorate in Detroit, along with other Baptists, my sense of church was small. The intervening years have seen it grow large. This growth in a sense of church has lessened my Baptist loyalty not one whit. After representing our denomination at Amsterdam, I see more clearly than ever the need for the Baptist and the free church witness to: soul liberty, evangelism, the regenerate church membership, and separation between church and state. The World Council of Churches will be less than a world council apart from what Baptists and free churchmen have to offer. There is still a loyalty to our Baptist churches, but there is a greater loyalty to the church universal.

In recent years it has been my privilege to serve on the theological section of the study commission for the International Council of Religious Education and on the Committee on the Witness of the Church for the Federal (now National) Council of Churches. These firsthand experiences have shown me that sectarians or any others concerned about the orthodoxy of the church need have no fear of heresy in the ecumenical movement. God knows how to care for the faith once for all delivered.

A bit of autobiography may be of interest to help account for the growth in appreciation of the larger loyalty. My ecumenical views would not be as wide apart from my close contact with Christians of other bodies, especially those of the Disciples of Christ. In looking backward, I see that it was my college roommate and fellow minister, Adiel Moncrief, who introduced me to the *Christian Century,* with whom the process of enlargement began. Edgar Fay Daugherty, minister of the Jackson Street Christian Church of Muncie, accelerated the process. I shall never forget going with him to DePauw University. It was an ecumenical gathering; I have forgotten its precise nature, but will always remember the impression made upon me by Bromley Oxnam, then president of the University, now Bishop of the Methodist Church and one of the Presidents of the World Council of Churches. A year later we went together to the Student Volunteer Meeting in Indianapolis, where I was both thrilled and challenged by the magnificent figure of William Temple. When I moved to Detroit, Edgar

DeWitt Jones, my colleague three blocks north on Woodward Avenue, gave meaningful encouragement to a young preacher. Working intimately on committees of the Northern Baptist Convention toward a closer relation with Disciples of Christ has widened my horizons and given me an intimate knowledge of another Christian body. As I have grown to know and love men of another fold, I have seen increasingly that they are not of another fold, but that we are all of one fold and there is one Shepherd.

Ten years have witnessed the vertical dimension strengthened and the horizontal broadened, the Bible is more than ever the Word of the living God, and Jesus Christ, the Son of God and our Saviour, is seen ever more clearly as the one hope for mankind.